Teens

Talk

About

Mental Health

by Leanne Kabat & Angela Kim

ISBN Number: 978-1-7335410-4-6

Published by Leanne Kabat Media

Please reach Leanne Kabat at 5seasonslife.com

Please reach Angela Kim at angelakimconsulting.com

Also by Leanne Kabat

The 5 Seasons of Connection to Your Child
The 5 Seasons of Connection to Your Love Partner
The 5 Seasons of Connection to Your Business Brilliance

Table of Contents

Part I

By trying various strategies to better ourselves, and sharing our experiences about what we went through, we're giving the readers a raw view about mental health and how we can take the initiative to better ourselves. We're able to show that we're not embarrassed or afraid of showing the world that everybody goes through mental health problems. By doing that, slowly but surely, we're breaking down the stigma against mental health for everyone.

~ Samantha Sy-Perez,
teen author in the IMPACT Project

Introduction

Search the term, 'mental health' online and you will find 2.8 billion results. Everyone has their own ideas about what it means, and with various media outlets, celebrities, politicians, researchers, and influencers using the term to explain vastly different concepts, we aren't always talking about the same thing.

While physical health relates to our whole body, mental health is about how our mind deals with feelings, understandings, and processing experiences such as anxiety, happiness, anger, or sadness, and the thoughts and emotions we have as a result. Good mental health enables people to cope with the stresses of life, realize their abilities, relate to others, learn continuously, work effectively, make healthy choices, and contribute to their community.

If we think about physical and mental health as two sides of the same coin for humans, it would seem that we can evaluate them both openly and objectively. I mean, if someone had heart disease or cancer, we would talk about it at work or our kid's soccer game. In 2020, 550 million people were living with heart disease, and 18 million people developed cancer. While those are large numbers, one other statistic dwarfs them both. In 2020, the World Health Organization released a study that stated 1.26 billion people in the world are living with mental health issues, including 75 million children and teens. Anxiety and depressive disorders are the most common conditions.

If one in eight people on the planet are struggling with their mental health, why isn't everyone talking about it?

For much of history, in many cultures, poor mental health has been treated as evidence of personal failure, points of shame, and embarrassing parts of ourselves that we should hide. For some cultures, this is still the case today. The stigma around mental health is prevalent in the workforce, in the health industry, in social circles, and in schools.

Teens are often the hardest hit with mental stress and overwhelm because they don't have the life skills or experience to move through various issues, and they lack the confidence to ask for help or support. Oftentimes, they internalize their stress and struggle as personal failures, and refuse to get help because they see that as labeling themselves weak and incapable. So, invertedly, they keep the stigma against mental health, stress, overwhelm, and struggle going.

Reading an article or a study about the mental health crisis for teens is one thing, seeing it play out in front of you is something quite different. We both work with teens, and we saw the negative impact of stress on their mental health, as well as their reluctance to open up and talk about their experience. We were inspired to create a safe space and build a community of teens where we could start breaking down the walls of stigma against mental health.

As part of our commitment to having open and honest conversations with the teens through our work, we shared real stories about mental health, actively listened to their experiences, and provided guidance and options for their consideration. For many of our teens, they had never discussed mental health issues with other people before or normalized mental health topics through conversations with peers.

Forming this community through the creation of the IMPACT Project was integral to breaking down the bias against mental health, challenging mental health myths, and introducing the students to many possible ways to manage and maintain positive mental health.

We don't talk about mental health enough, we don't ask enough questions of teens to find out their lived experience, and to understand what support they need to feel strong and confident to face any storm that comes their way.

We started this program to change the conversation around stress, overwhelm, and mental health, and to help end our students' struggles of keeping their emotions hidden because of embarrassment, fear, or shame. The stigma around mental health keeps teens, and millions of others, feeling isolated, disconnected, and dealing with all their emotions on their own.

We are here to change all this, and so much more.

Leanne Kabat & Angela Kim

CHAPTER 1

Why We Need IMPACT

By Leanne Kabat

A wild and wonderful collection of university students came together from all parts of Canada to live on campus in the nation's capital city. I was a new Resident Assistant (RA), and my two main responsibilities were helping students bond so they could build a strong support network to help them navigate their first year of university life and keep them safe. I supported them when they were falling in love and then out of love. I was there when they struggled to keep up with the demands of their academic programs and the times they fell apart. I helped them with homesickness and hopelessness - sometimes at the same time.

James was a first year student. On move-in day, his parents asked me all the usual questions and then they translated my answers for him. When all the parents left to go back home, his parents were the last to leave. Over the next few days, I held some ice-breakers and community-building activities. Even though I waved him in, he often sat at the back of the room and watched everyone else without participating. In the lounge one night, I was listening to music when James came in and sat beside me. I asked how he was doing, and when he didn't answer, I thought he might not understand me. Then he spoke and his English was perfect. He wasn't sure how he was doing; he was feeling out of place. I asked why he hadn't joined in on any of the floor bonding activities as they were designed to help facilitate friendships, and he said his parents wouldn't want him to participate, he was only there to study.

Over the course of the next few months, James would often work beside me in the study room or join me in the lounge to do complex math homework while I watched whatever was on TV. While other students asked how to get downtown or where to find the best pizza, James would quietly ask me how I thought people could fix their weaknesses, or how to do everything right all the time, or how to stop being a failure. As a budding journalism student, I peppered him with questions to dig deeper into why those thoughts were on his mind, but he never answered any questions, he only asked them. Although he seemed to be a deeply private person, I could feel that a part of him wanted to connect with other people; he just kept stopping himself. The only other person he had a bond with was his roommate Manu.

James struggled in the first few months. He felt lost in his intro classes where he sat in auditoriums of three hundred students, so he attended every extra tutoring session available and frequently went to his professor's office hours. I often saw him in the study lounge until the wee hours, sometimes asleep on his books. I told him I was worried about him many times, and that his recent weight loss, acne flare ups, and chronic sniffles could be signs of extreme stress. He brushed me off as being more of a mom than an RA, but I watched him closely. By our December break, he said his grades were not what he wanted them to be, and he seemed apprehensive about going home. When he returned in January, he was more dedicated to his schoolwork than ever before.

It was a particularly dark and stormy February that year. With Spring Break fast approaching, the energy on our floor shifted from gloomy to giddy. Most students were buzzing about flying south for some sun and fun, but James wanted to stay in residence. I asked why he didn't want to go home, but he said he had too much to do. A handful of other students in our dorm house also remained in residence, including James' roommate. I also stayed, happily taking advantage of the empty broadcast studio to complete some big projects.

One stormy winter night, I was working late in the studio when I heard someone yelling my name in the hallway. I jumped up and opened the studio door to find Manu there, panicked and screaming James' name over and over. I tried to find out more, but he couldn't speak. I grabbed my keys and raced back to our floor. I ran through the blinding snow and sleet of the winter storm to get to our residence and James' room. Their door was open, but the bathroom was locked. I could hear moaning inside and I called out James' name. By this time, Manu caught up with me, huffing and puffing. He managed to blurt out, "there's a lot of blood."

I knocked hard at first, then softly, while calling out James' name over and over. Finally, my voice broke through his cries, and he called out, "Leanne, is that you?"

"Yes, I'm here. Can you unlock the door?" I asked.

"I'm not in good shape, I'm not in good shape," he kept saying.

"I can handle you in any shape, but not from out here. You have to let me in," I pleaded. I told Manu to run to the main building to call an ambulance. In the winter storm we were having, I knew it would take a while.

James unlocked the bathroom door and let me in, then quickly locked it behind me. He stood there in the bathtub in only a pair of shorts, holding a piece of broken glass that he was using to cut himself all over. Manu was right, there was a lot of blood. James reached for my hand and held it tightly as he collapsed into the tub, sobbing hard and sharing his deepest fears.

I'm such a failure.
I let my parents down.
They sacrificed everything.
They deserve a better son than me.
For once, I wish I wasn't such a failure.

He said his grades were in the low B range, even though he had tried so hard. He said his parents had told him to not come home until he had A's.

James was buckling under the pressure of an impossible situation and now he was emotionally broken, physically bleeding, and nearing the point of no return. I applied pressure to his bigger wounds with a towel I found on the floor, praying the ambulance would arrive quickly. We stayed in the bathtub for nearly an hour, crying, talking, telling stories, and sharing secrets. When the paramedics finally arrived, they carefully guided James out of the tub and onto the waiting gurney. They strapped him down and raced away into the dark, cold winter night. I never saw James again. His family arranged for his things to be shipped home, and Manu finished the year without his roommate. Manu and I talked about James often, breaking down our experiences to find clues that would help us understand what he was experiencing, and how we might have let him down.

I've thought about James many times over the years, wondering what happened after he left me that night. Throughout my life, I have worked with hundreds of students, and I am always looking for the signs that tell me how deeply they are hurting, or how close to their edge they might be – signs I might have missed thirty years ago with James. I mean, I had seen the surface signs: weight loss, lethargy, acne, isolation, and anxiousness, but I didn't see what pushed him over the edge that night. I didn't know for sure what became his breaking point.

After two decades of teaching, training, and coaching teens and young adults, I now believe that we can never really know what pushes people to their breaking point because it is different for every person, and it is different every time. Something that might feel catastrophic one day might be a big-yet-conquerable obstacle another day. Someone might get through a big trauma and compartmentalize it so they can keep going but be devastated by something others might consider 'minor.'

Our capacity to deal with hard things, and our personal resources that we can tap into to deal with hard things is fluid, and can change depending on so many factors, like:

- how many decisions we had already made in a day,
- what the negative voice in our minds is telling us,
- who we might be afraid of disappointing,
- the level of stress we are already under,
- how much/little sleep we have had,
- being hungry or dehydrated,
- feeling sad, angry, afraid.

We all face storms in our lives. Sometimes they are caused by internal stressors, sometimes they are caused by external ones. Replace the word 'storm' for any of the big challenges in our lives, such as:

- failing a test
- losing your job
- being betrayed
- hurting a friend
- breaking a bone
- making a mistake
- being in a car accident
- disappointing loved ones
- having your identity stolen
- doing something you really regret
- knowing *right* and *wrong* and choosing 'wrong'
- opening a rejection letter from your dream school

We have seen this in our families, in our communities, and even on television when celebrities unexpectedly 'snap,' and they behave in an explosively negative way that they later deeply regret. It's rarely about the incident we see unfold in front of us, it's almost always about a long-festering hurt emotion or unresolved issue from a previous time that has been living inside of them until the moment it bursts out.

Oftentimes, we push those experiences out of our minds, but since we're the sum of every single thought, action, interaction, feeling, and experience we've ever had, we carry every trouble, triumph, sadness, and success in our cells. These can surface and create an emotional storm after months, years, or even decades.

We can't prevent storms from coming into our lives, but we can control who we are when the storms hit, and how long we suffer before we try something different. This is where our personal power lies.

At the core of my work lies one unshakable truth: when we know who we are in every season, we are better equipped to face every test, trial, trouble, or traumatic experience with self-compassion and strength. It doesn't mean what is happening to us isn't hard, it just means we don't have to stay trapped in the 'hard.'

With life moving at break-neck speed again after the global pandemic, we are all just trying to keep up with the demands, expectations, and pressures coming from all angles. There is an urgency that we have to catch up, make up for lost time, and be better than we ever were before to show we didn't 'lose' the last two years.

Now, imagine you are doing all this at fifteen years old.

Developmentally, you are entering a period of your life where there are slightly more demands and obligations than before, and it is the time for you to establish social and emotional habits for mental well-being, like building strong friend relationships, prioritizing healthy habits around sleep, exercise, and eating, strengthening your problem-solving and conflict-management skills, and experimenting with healthy ways to get your needs met. Often without realizing it, teens are also setting the foundation for how they deal with pressure, stress, overwhelm, and conflict, now and in their future. We hope the practices and habits they build are healthy and helpful for their growth, happiness, and success, but the teen years are also a time for more independence and freedom, so they want to do it on their own.

However, we are coming out of one of the most tumultuous times in recent history and our healthy habits and wellness practices have been weakened. Many families are hurting, friendships are strained, social gatherings and celebrations are still being canceled, and the academic pressure to make up for lost time over the past two years is intense. Remote learning was extremely challenging for many students and teachers, and learning and engagement was severely impacted.

As a fifteen-year-old, you are feeling disconnected from friends, sad and grieving the loss of your sports, clubs, programs, jobs, opportunities, parties, and traditions, and scrambling to get into a good college in a few years.

So, you push yourself to learn everything you possibly can from six or seven completely different teachers in completely different subjects, and consistently demonstrate how much you know in every assignment, test, exam, and presentation. You work hard to check all the boxes for successful college admission like taking all the right classes at the most rigorous levels, getting the highest grades, adding in the best extracurriculars that help you stand out, acing the standardized tests, writing compelling and original essays, and securing exceptional letter of recommendation. You are happy to be back in competitive sports, but you're not the player you used to be, so you must work extra hard to get back in shape. And helping with siblings, doing chores, and serving others is still expected of you. Let's not forget, some communities are still experiencing school closures, remote learning, and policies that keep changing. With your friends' schedules as hectic as yours, you resort to saying '*hi*' in the hallways at school and connecting online at night. We all know relationships online aren't the same as relationships in person, so loneliness and social emptiness start to bring you down. But you can't spend time worrying about it because you are already worrying about everything else, so you cut back on sleep because there isn't enough time in your day, and the upward stress cycle starts.

When we are in the stress cycle, small things become big things, and we lose track of what brings us joy, what we are capable of doing, and what resources we can access to make it easier for us.

When Angela and I started talking about the rising stress cycle in our communities, we were shocked by the findings of studies examining how the state of teens' mental health has changed in both a post-soaring social media habit and a post-COVID-19 world. After both shifts in our culture, researchers reported on the sharp rise in the rates of depression, anxiety, panic symptoms, and self-harm in children and teens across the country and around the world. We looked at the statistics and decided we had to do something to better support teens in our communities, but we didn't want to presume to know what they needed, so we brainstormed how we could figure it out.

From our research, we found a lot of confusing information about the most effective strategies, and very little data on effectiveness for teens, in particular. While mindfulness is often the top recommended tip, we couldn't find one clear path of what mindfulness looks like for teens, or what options there are when someone wants to try something other than meditation.

I'm a teacher, instructional designer, researcher, and author, and Angela is a college counselor and leadership trainer with a full client roster of teens. Looking at our skills, we had more than enough expertise to create a comprehensive project to research what techniques would be most helpful to teens, and we invited Angela's students to participate. We hoped a few of them would be interested in our program to examine and experiment with various ways to reduce stress and struggle and break the stigma around mental health for teens. Every one of her students signed up.

For me, it was critical that we created a community first, having ice breakers and open discussions so each student could build trust and safety with each other. Every week, we all shared our wins and cool things that happened to become a part of each other's celebrations and successes. Sometimes the shares were big, like winning a sports tournament or acing a test, but oftentimes we heard about the small or simple wins that they might not have shared with friends or family, like getting a good night's sleep for once, or talking with their grandma on the phone. The act of sharing and the art of listening helped show each of us that we are not alone in our lived experiences. As the weeks went on, the students' confidence grew, and the discussions were even more open, honest, and authentic.

We were not fully prepared for how deeply they craved this kind of community, and how quickly they stepped into the learning and development opportunities we provided. By participating in the weekly challenges and engaging in our leadership training sessions, they were able to test their limits, stretch their comfort zone, try new things in a nurturing and supportive environment, and find the strategies that would serve them best. Although they told us many times about how much they were getting from the program to strengthen their mindset, improve their stress management and leadership skills, and identify a customized collection of tools to help them move through their hard times, they weren't the only ones who received incredible gifts.

Angela and I also received many gifts throughout our time together, and the most rewarding one as a mentor was to witness each student's transformation over the course of five months. We were honored to hear their thoughts and feelings in our discussion groups, read their words in their reflections, and know their experiences from their stories - which you will see in their chapters later in this book. Through this project, they found their strength, they released some of the beliefs that had been holding them back, and they stepped into their authenticity and vulnerability as the leaders we know they are.

I feel so proud of these students as they graduate from the IMPACT Project and know how to take everything they have discovered about themselves and their strengths and confidently live a life they love. Yet, it's a bittersweet moment for me as well. Even after three decades, I can't help but think about my former university student James, and how much he would have benefited from having an opportunity to find his strengths, learn new stress management skills, step into his own leadership style, and find the courage to ask for help before his overwhelm and silent suffering brought him to his breaking point. I don't know where he is in the world right now, but as I watch our IMPACT students soar, I am so grateful that he taught me how to keep an open heart and a willing spirit to partner with every person I coach so they feel seen, heard, validated, celebrated, and supported on their journey to discover who they are and what they can create with their unique gifts to make the world a better place.

About the Author

Leanne Kabat

Leanne Kabat is the author of several books in her *5 Seasons of Connection* collection and an international speaker/trainer. Her first book helps overwhelmed parents connect with their kids on a deeper level; her second book guides couples out of conflict and towards their most intimate connection; and her third book helps purpose-driven entrepreneurs overcome fears of success and failure to build a profitable business on their brilliance. She has taught her 5 Seasons framework to families, couples, and entrepreneurs in dozens of countries, including Uganda, South Africa, Austria, Australia, Canada, and the U.S.

Leanne is currently working towards her master's degree in Social and Emotional Learning to continue making transformational change with her students and clients. She recently earned a Women in Leadership Certificate from Cornell University to build upon her undergraduate degrees in Education and Journalism.

Leanne found her passion for social and emotional health through the creation of her 5 Seasons framework. She relied on her own teachings in 2006 when she fell ill and was given five years to live. Sixteen years later, she is thriving in the Pacific Northwest with her family, and excited to visit her 57th country when it's safe to do so.

To discover how the 5 Seasons can change your life, love, or business, please visit 5seasonslife.com or email Leanne directly at info@5seasonslife.com.

CHAPTER 2

How We Make IMPACT

By Angela Kim

As a college counselor and leadership training coach, I have seen the ups and downs of many teens during their high school years. I've celebrated when they aced their tests, sailed through their SAT exams, and received acceptance letters from their dream schools. I have also consoled them when they failed a test, missed a deadline, or had a falling out with a friend. Over the past few years, academic, social, and emotional pressure on students has been steadily increasing, but nothing prepared me for watching them handle the mental stress and struggle of life in a post-COVID world.

Sixteen-year old John said, "I really don't know how to keep up anymore. All of these pressures at school are just too much. I probably won't get into any college anyways. Do you think I should just go to the army instead?"

David's mom called me in a panic. She shared that her fifteen-year old had locked himself in his room with the lights off for five days, refusing to talk to anyone. She left food outside his door and picked up the empty dishes later in the evening but couldn't get him to come out. One month later, David was diagnosed with major depression.

Ashley's relentless procrastination meant she lived in a constant state of anger or dread. She raged if she scored less than 94 percent on anything, and even a 99 percent wasn't good enough. She was staying up later than 1 A.M. to study harder, and still getting up at 6:30 in the morning to get to school on time. She was sleep-deprived, exhausted, and snapping at her friends and family.

Everyone commented how Jessica was like the Energizer Bunny because she was involved in everything. At one point, she was a member of three clubs, president of her own club, participated in after school sports, had piano, math and English tutoring during the week, was studying for her SAT on Saturdays, and she volunteered at the animal shelter on Sundays. Her schedule was so busy, she often skipped breakfast and ate lunch in her car. Even with a crammed schedule, she struggled with extreme anxiety and felt she was never doing enough to participate in her extracurricular activities to get into college.

For the past eight years, I have been working closely with teens as a college and career counselor and have witnessed their academic, emotional, and mental successes and struggles. My top priority with my students is to create a safe, welcoming, and supportive environment so they can be vulnerable, open, and authentic with me. Within this space, many of them feel safe to confide in me about their struggles, their emotional distress, their feelings of failure, or frustration managing all the pressure that is on their shoulders.

It's not that students haven't always faced obstacles in their high school years, but I believe the experience of current students is significantly more challenging than in previous years. This generation of high school students actually started elementary school after Instagram, Snapchat, and Facebook were already changing the way people talked, shared, and connected around the world; they don't know life without social media and likes, shares, tweets, or language like LOL or IRL (*Laugh Out Loud* and *In Real Life*).

The Soaring Costs of a College Education in the Post-COVID-19 Landscape

Over the years, admission to college has changed dramatically compared to what it was even twenty years ago. The turmoil of college admissions has caused a sense of panic among students and parents.

The cost of college has risen five times faster than family incomes over the past ten years, and the costs keep rising each year. Meanwhile, as the value of a college degree rose, the number of applicants surged, yet the number of students admitted declined at the top schools. As most colleges across the country are seeing the same surge in demand and drop in supply, students are facing intense competition to earn a coveted spot.

To stay competitive, most students will take the most demanding classes, keep A grades, perform at their best in every quiz, project, and exam, take on leadership roles, participate in a wide variety of extracurricular activities, play an instrument, participate in a sport, help with chores and household tasks, manage a part-time job to help save for college, and not waste any time.

COVID-19 added a new layer of complexity. Students had to master remote-learning strategies, earn points and be tested in new and unfamiliar ways, navigate shifting political and medical priorities, while watching their clubs, teams, and activities shut down completely. Yet, despite these closures, the pressures of college still remain the same.

There is yet another layer we need to consider when examining the journey of high school students working towards a positive college outcome, and that is the role of culture.

The Role of Culture

Culture is an umbrella term that refers to a large collection of accepted values, beliefs, languages, religions, customs, laws, and habits of a specific group, often from a specific region. It is learned and shared from parent to child, friend to friend, and it becomes a part of our unconscious understanding of the world we live in.

While every culture has positive and negative aspects, some have traditions and values that were designed to be positive but can become detrimental to its people when things are taken too far. This is the case in South Korea.

South Korea is incredible in many ways, yet it is also a country whose population is severely overworked and over-anxious. It is a nation that is on the verge of a social and emotional breakdown evidenced by high divorce rates, the highest ranking for having the unhappiest children among OECD countries, and one of the highest suicide rates among developed nations.

Mental Health Stigma Entrenched in Korean Culture

While there are many factors for this tragedy, there are two main reasons.

1. Historical Stigma Against Mental Health

   The negative perception of this issue is so deeply rooted in Korean culture that throughout most of its history, the existence of mental stressors or mental illnesses has been denied and denounced. Even now, people are discouraged from accessing mental health services as many insurance companies don't cover mental health appointments, or if they do, the person's medical record is permanently labeled with a specific code that prevents them from changing insurance companies, or even having certain jobs in healthcare or in the government. While neighboring Japan spends $130 million each year on suicide prevention and awareness campaigns, South Korea spends $7 million, with most of that money going to hospitals delivering treatments and not on prevention or awareness.

2. Social Shame Against Mental Health

   As a nation that was historically oppressed, generations of Koreans have struggled to protect their cultural identity while working hard to become strong and independent. Many families have a "survivor mentality" and powered through every obstacle and barrier they faced without showing any signs of struggle to the outside world. Even today, embedded in the culture is the expectation that Koreans must work hard to move forward and not let feelings or emotions get in the way. Silence is a sign of strength; talking about emotions is a sign of weakness.

Knowing this history, it makes sense how the Korean culture views people suffering from mental or emotional illnesses as shameful or a failure. It takes a lot of courage or pain for someone to admit they need mental health support for they know their entire family might experience embarrassment and shame for having a weak person in the family. This person would be seen as broken, flawed, or an outcast. These negative beliefs show how deeply entrenched the stigma is that having mental health issues equates to shaming and disappointing their family and perhaps even their community.

Korea is experiencing a mental health crisis. But we wanted to ask, how do these deeply-rooted, culturally entrenched stigmas against mental health affect teens in particular?

Each generation learned to suppress or ignore their emotions, and those behaviors were passed onto every following generation. Children grow up hiding and controlling their emotions because that's how their parents were brought up. As a result, many Korean teens do not know how they feel and cannot identify many 'feeling words.' They go through life working hard day after day without really feeling and evaluating situations based on their emotions. This is evident in my work when I coach students. I often ask how they feel about something, and they struggle to come up with answers every time so it is clear to me their emotional muscles have not been developed. It makes sense, then, that when they feel stress or overwhelm, they don't know how to handle it. And, because they haven't seen their parents or other members of their family or community deal with emotions or stress, many teens resort to unhealthy habits like overeating, numbing out by gaming for hours, or screaming into their pillows. They become accustomed to stuffing their emotional distress until it often reaches a devastating boiling point.

Why Teenagers Are At Such a High Risk: The Boiling Academic Pressure

For Korean children, this culturally instilled stigma against mental health turns into subconscious beliefs right from childhood. The pressures on Korean students to always perform in the zone of academic excellence are relentless, and it doesn't just affect students when they become teens. Chronic stress and unhappiness from intense academic pressures begin at a very young age with children going to after-school programs until late every night, and high school students staying up to do schoolwork well past midnight, taking extra classes on weekends and during the summer.

In the Korean culture, teens regularly hear about the importance of getting the highest test scores and best grades as the ticket to getting into the best college and having a good future. For these students, being less than perfect means that they failed, and the implications of their failure (in many cases having a B in a class) signals that their family has failed. So, their sole focus becomes academic excellence at any emotional, mental, or physical cost. When students do not achieve their goals, exceed expectations, or maintain perfect performance, they often feel they have dishonored their families so profoundly, some feel they have no other choice but to stop being a burden, no matter how hard they have to work. Their feelings of guilt, fear of shame, fear of seeming weak, and fear of failure pushes them to drown in academic pressure and suffer in silence.

This is the state of mental health in Korea. Now, how does this translate to teens in the U.S.? The third and final added layer that we must consider is immigration.

Entanglement of Mental Health and Immigration

One might think that culture, values, beliefs, traditions, and customs all change when families immigrate to the U.S., but families stay connected to their culture regardless of their geography. Research shows that it isn't just where you were born or raised, it has to do with how deeply entrenched your parents and family hold tight to the values and traditions of their culture.

As a Korean American, born in Korea myself, my values and beliefs have been shaped by the long-standing traditions and customs from our culture, even though I haven't lived there in over twenty years. Regardless of how long I have been in the U.S., I have personally felt the intense pressure to perform at the highest levels and I have seen the punishing stigma of Korean people hiding their mental health struggles to not bring shame and dishonor to their family.

In the Korean American culture, it is still customary to not show any signs of weakness because we all strive to achieve success at any costs. Like some other Asian cultures, Koreans live under the "model minority" stereotype, where people try to live up to the expectations of their culture. According to the University of Texas at Austin's Counseling and Mental Health Center, the 'model minority' sets the stereotype that Asian Americans will have certain unalienable characteristics, such as being good at math, science, and technology, as well as being hardworking, wealthy, and self-sufficient. In order to meet this expectation, mental health concerns are ignored because they either get in the way or are still seen as a sign of weakness, an excuse, or a waste of time.

As a result, for many Korean American students, the pressure on teens becomes magnified when students identify as coming from first or second generation immigrant families. Their parents sacrificed so much to immigrate to the U.S. to give them a better future and because of this, the first generation pressure on students to perform and do well is immense. The costs are staggering for families, and they can't afford to make a mistake.

And this isn't just the case for students in Korean or even some Asian cultures. Other immigrant cultures have their own traditions, values, and beliefs which impact their high school and college-bound journeys.

All of my current students in this project are first and second generation immigrants. While most of my students are Korean Americans, I have had the pleasure over the years of coaching and consulting with students from other cultures too, including American and Mexican. Two of my current Mexican students shared this about the pressure on them to succeed academically.

In Mexican culture, there is a heavy cultural pressure to succeed academically to then succeed financially to support your family. No matter what, whatever you do or become is to provide for your family. That's why so many families from Mexico immigrate to the United States; they seek a better way of living and more opportunities.

For instance, one Mexican peso amounts to $0.049 US dollars. So, for our generation of Mexican students, we are encouraged to go to college because we will make more money than if we dropped out of high school to go to work at a young age. By going to college, we will have the life our parents wished us to have, and we won't have to walk through their path of devastating hardships and crushing obstacles.

In our culture, there are many pressures on young people to get into college and have a great job, and as we are working hard to do that, we can't ever show feelings of depression or anxiety because we are supposed to focus on our responsibilities to care for our younger siblings, help our grandparents, work part-time jobs, and to contribute to our family.

If we give up or stop working hard because of mental stress or overwhelm, we're indirectly also giving up on our family because dropping out of school or quitting our job affects the life we want to give our family. Our culture sees struggle as a way to persevere in order to reach fulfillment and bring our family out of poverty or have a place to live for our kids. But this pressure at home is on top of pressure at school, and it gets really hard sometimes.

There aren't many open, honest conversations or support for mental health in our culture or in our families. If mental health is brought up, the parents often get defensive because they don't think the child had it worse than they did. The conversation then turns into an argument, or it is dismissed to be somebody else's problem.

Because it is a closed topic, most of us don't understand if we are experiencing depression, anxiety, panic attacks, or other mental illnesses. And since time is so tight, we think that taking care of ourselves is a waste of time because we have so much to accomplish and so much to worry about.

For students from the Mexican cultures too, mental health had no place in their life. In a broader sense, to varying degrees, this is the unfortunate reality of mental struggles among many immigrant cultures. For first and second generation immigrant students in particular, the combination of excruciating academic pressure and the association of mental illness with weakness and shame have come together to create the perfect storm of anguish and suffering.

They feel the pressure that their parents immigrated to the States in search of a better life for them and their family, so they strongly believe getting the highest test scores and best grades are the ticket to getting into the best college and having a good and secured future.

And even without considering the layer of culture and immigration, mental health is a universal problem among many teens today in the U.S.

According to the report, *The State Of Mental Health In America 2022*, published by Mental Health America, and the CDC report in 2021, teens are experiencing a mental health crisis in the United States. Here are some statistics that illuminate this crisis:

- 15% of youth (12-17) experience depression.
- 2.5 million youth in the U.S. have severe depression.
- Over 60% of youth with major depression do not receive any mental health treatment.
- 44% of high school students reported they felt sad or hopeless almost every day during the past year and stopped doing things they enjoyed.
- 38% of youth experience anxiety disorders, totaling 15.8 million teens from age 10-19.
- 70% of public schools reported an increase in the number of students seeking mental health services between 2020 and 2022.

Regardless of the culture or the geography of a student, teen mental health is in crisis. We have the research to back it up, but anyone who is a teen, has a teen, or knows a teen will know it is true.

When I Decided to Be Part of the Solution

Over the years in my college and career planning work, I would meet with students and behind their polite smile, I could see in their eyes the same perfectionist behavior, the same deep exhaustion, and the same intense fear of failing their family. More recently, with the added pressure of what is happening in today's college environment with increased competition, decreased admittance rates, and soaring costs, the situation has never been more dire.

When I was working with my students on their college essays or on designing their college lists, I often thought how it seemed like they were not just juggling, but juggling flaming torches. I tried to come up with ideas on how to support, motivate, and cheer them up. How could I encourage them more? How could I help them realize that there is a light at the end of this seemingly endless dark tunnel? How could I help them get through this extra-stressful season of their life preparing for their college admissions with more ease and purpose? These thoughts haunted me night after night. I couldn't do anything about their pressure or workload, but I felt like I had to do 'something.'

Then one random Thursday night, I realized that 'something' was helping with *how* they manage their pressure and workload. I came across an article that said, "Join our 30-day mental health challenge." An idea started to form. Excited and hopeful, I reached out to my business coach and mentor, Leanne, and we started to brainstorm possibilities. As a former teacher, she knew about students, and as an expert with course structure and curriculum design, I knew we could create something amazing, and we did.

Interconnected Minds Positively Affecting Communities Together, or the IMPACT Project, became a tool for self-awareness, self-empowerment, and personal and professional growth for my current cohort of high school students. Through the design of our program, we were able to help eleven students stretch and grow in their skills and knowledge around mental health and wellness, having dynamic discussions about self-care strategies, personal development, and our circle of control, exploring what things are in our control, and what things are outside of our control. By creating a safe space for them to try new things and share their experiences in a group of their peers, they saw they are not alone. It was my dream to create a leadership program that incorporated conversations around mental health so together, we could break the stigma around stress, struggle, and overwhelm. One of the outcomes of seeing how transformational the IMPACT Project has been to our students is to imagine how many more people could benefit from the program; we fully embraced the philosophy, 'impact yourself, impact the world.'

When I was a university student, I believed that we went to college in the pursuit of happiness and success. However, the definition of success has changed over the years, and many people see college as the only way to secure a high-paying job, while paying little to no regard for happiness. From my years of experience in my community and in my industry, a college education and well-paying career does not guarantee happiness; what really increases someone's level of happiness is our mindset and the state of our mental health. Ultimately, this is why I wanted to create the IMPACT Project.

However, it isn't just happiness I want to teach my students, because happiness is not a permanent state of mind. I also believe in the importance and power of having strong leadership skills. A leader is not made because they hold a title; a leader is made when someone nurtures a collection of skills that allows them to contribute to others, take ownership and responsibility, and move towards their vision. I wanted to create a platform and opportunities for my students to unleash the leader within them.

In the following pages, you will see some of our process, and then hear from the teens in our program. Each student will share four stories of their most memorable challenges, as well as words of wisdom.

In Part III, we will hear their stories.

About the Author
Angela Kim

Angela Kim is a college counselor and leadership trainer. For the past eight years, she has channeled her passion for personal and professional growth to help teens and young adults find their strengths and use them to build a successful future. She has helped dozens of students get admitted to the college of their dreams.

While working with teens, Angela saw first-hand the emotional struggles, pressure, and stress they faced. Believing that mental health is the most important factor for personal development and success, she founded the IMPACT Project to give students the skills to lead with confidence in today's world.

She received her B.A. in Psychology from UCLA and a College Access Counseling Certification from Rice University. Angela is also a John Maxwell Certified Speaker, Trainer, and Coach who has been a speaker for National Geographic and Cal State Fullerton.

Angela is happily married to her husband, and in their free time, they enjoy attending concerts and playing with their Maltese dog, Benji. She loves feeding her Thai food obsession and exploring the local restaurant scene.

For more information about the IMPACT Project or her college and career services, please visit www.angelakimconsulting.com or email Angela directly at info@angelakimconsulting.com.

Part II

CHAPTER 3

The IMPACT Research Project

Before we launched the project, we identified many mental health and wellness techniques that we could test, but we wanted to also discover what categories of wellness were most helpful to our students, and other teens as well. We set up four broad categories to study: Mindfulness, Joyful Positivity, Connection with Others, and Physical Activity. Under each category, we itemized four or five specific tests the students could complete so we could see what exact strategies were best, and what bigger categories created the most notable change. We turned each strategy into a *'challenge'* where the students would learn how to complete the activity, and then challenge themselves to practice it daily.

We had several objectives:

1. We wanted to test a wide range of strategies.

    Just as everyone has their own personality type, learning style, perspective, temperament, and goals, each one of our students has their own unique response to every challenge, and not all challenges are as effective or empowering for everyone. Plus, different challenges satisfy different aspects of mental, emotional, or physical wellness so variety was key.

2. We wanted to include challenges that pushed them out of their comfort zone.

    Developmentally, teens are ready to become more independent. Some teens are quick to try new things, while others would rather observe and then decide if they wanted to jump in. It was important to create a safe, supported environment for them to test their own limits and push the boundaries of their comfort zone so they could see what they are capable of on their own.

3. We wanted to make it quick and easy.

   Except for one longer challenge, every daily challenge lasted from one to three minutes, once or twice a day. We ran this program through the school year and didn't want to add stress or take time away from their schoolwork or other commitments.

4. We wanted to go deeper than surface-level.

   We didn't include challenges that were designed to make them feel nice, like pampering sessions or mindless activities. We selected challenges that had the potential to bring them deeper into self-awareness, to change their perspective, or to teach them something new.

5. We wanted to offer professional and personal growth training.

   As the workforce is shifting, most people in this generation of teens will find they are expected to have strong leadership skills, regardless of their career. We wanted to take the opportunity to help them develop stronger skills they will need to succeed, like more effective communication, problem-solving, and analysis, as well as helping them want to become a lifelong learner, and challenging limiting beliefs.

6. We wanted to encourage a growth-mindset for wellness.

   At this stage, teens don't need to know *what* to think but *how* to think. How can they see a problem in a new way? How can they select the best solution to fix their issue? What might they try that they had never tried before? Being open and flexible are hallmarks of having a growth mindset, but more importantly for teens are shifts like:

   - My brain is a muscle that can grow.
   - I can learn and practice taking educated risks.

- Mistakes as opportunities to do something differently.
- I can change the phrase, 'I can't do it,' to 'I can't do it *yet*' to allow for growth.

Growth-mindset is more than an objective, though. It is our driving passion. We both invest time and money into our own personal and professional development, but not everyone knows how much they can change their life by changing some of their thoughts, beliefs, and habits.

Teaching students about what they can control and what they can't control is life-changing; knowing what is in their zone of control helps dismantle some of the main causes of their anxieties. Some examples of their anxiety-inducing thoughts include catastrophic thinking (where they think if *one thing goes wrong*, their entire life is ruined), struggling with procrastination (while a complex issue, procrastination often masks perfectionism), and believing the 'one path lie,' (where they think 'there is only one path to a successful future, and I better find it and stay on it no matter what.').

With the pervasive power of social media, we wanted to ensure they received accurate information from reliable sources and give them an opportunity to explore plenty of tools to add to their mental and emotional toolbox for today, tomorrow, and their future. Our goal was never to say they would live a life of ease, or they would never face hard things. Our goal was to give them the knowledge, skills, abilities, and practice to move through every storm they faced with strength, grace, courage, and confidence. And during our program, when their storms hit, they made it through marvelously.

One barrier we wanted to overcome quickly was the newness of the group. The students came from seven cities and attended nine high schools, and only six knew each other before the start of the IMPACT Project. Our priority was to create trust and build community right away so they could get the most from the daily challenges and the weekly meetings, and we could get the most open and honest information from them about their true experience and the most precise measurements of the impact of each challenge.

The IMPACT Project Principles

Our Mission

To empower teens to step into leadership while integrating healthy, effective wellness practices so they can develop confidence, better manage stress and overwhelm, normalize mental health management, and make a positive impact for their future.

Our Vision

A world where teens and young adults explore and integrate healthy, effective, wellness practices to empower their growth in their mind, body, and soul.

Our Values

Leadership
Accountability
Respect & Integrity
Teamwork & Collaboration
Growth Mindset & Openness
Personal Development
Building Community
Full Participation
Having Fun

CHAPTER 4
The Data

When we set out to collect data, we were slightly apprehensive about the quantity and the quality of information we would be receiving from the students. After all, we had read studies about how challenging it was to get robust answers or accurate measurements from teens because they tended to perform tasks quickly and without much thought. We knew a key to overcoming this tendency was to make it real, relevant, and an opportunity for them to have full responsibility over their efforts and their results.

We collected data daily, and the students submitted their numerical results and extensive written reflections each week for the duration of the project.

We were sensitive to various external factors in their lives, such as high-stakes test days for AP exams and SAT, sports tournaments, extracurricular expectations, and family commitments, and we knew some days it might be easier to put any number down on the challenge form, but we insisted on accuracy, honesty, and integrity for the research collection. The students stepped up with thorough data collection, thoughtful reflections, and interesting insights in our meetings.

Here are the results:

Overview of the Challenges

Challenge	Challenge Name	Category
Challenge 1	Deep Breathing	Mindfulness
Challenge 2	Stretching Yoga	Physical Activity
Challenge 3	Compliment Someone	Connection to Others
Challenge 4	Create Joy List	Joyful Positivity
Challenge 5	Make Bed & Tidy Up	Joyful Positivity
Challenge 6	Air Boxing	Physical Activity
Challenge 7	5 Second Rule	Mindfulness
Challenge 8	Guided Meditation	Mindfulness
Challenge 9	Act of Kindness	Connection to Others
Challenge 10	Aerobic Exercise	Physical Activity
Challenge 11	How Others See Me	Connection to Others
Challenge 12	Be in Nature	Mindfulness
Challenge 13	Hold a Plank	Physical Activity
Challenge 14	Unplug Before Sleeping	Mindfulness
Challenge 15	Conversation Starters	Connection to Others
Challenge 16	Decluttering	Joyful Positivity
Challenge 17	Gratitude	Mindfulness
Challenge 18	Choose Your Own	Joyful Positivity

Challenges Ranked from Most Effective to Least Effective - All Students

Challenge #	Challenge Name	Category
Challenge 12	Be in Nature	Mindfulness
Challenge 18	Choose Your Own	Joyful Positivity
Challenge 17	Gratitude	Mindfulness
Challenge 14	Unplug Before Sleeping	Mindfulness
Challenge 10	Aerobic Exercise	Physical Activity
Challenge 11	How Others See Me	Connection to Others
Challenge 5	Make Bed & Tidy Up	Joyful Positivity
Challenge 16	Decluttering	Joyful Positivity
Challenge 8	Guided Meditation	Mindfulness
Challenge 13	Hold a Plank	Physical Activity
Challenge 1	Deep Breathing	Mindfulness
Challenge 15	Conversation Starters	Connection to Others
Challenge 7	5 Second Rule	Mindfulness
Challenge 9	Act of Kindness	Connection to Others
Challenge 6	Air Boxing	Physical Activity
Challenge 3	Compliment Someone	Connection to Others
Challenge 4	Create Joy List	Joyful Positivity
Challenge 2	Stretching Yoga	Physical Activity

Categories Ranked in Order of Most Effective to Least Effective - All Students

Top Category	Top Challenge in the Category
Mindfulness	Be in Nature
Connection to Others	How Others See Me
Joyful Positivity	Choose Your Own
Physical Activity	Aerobic Exercise

Challenges Ranked in Order of Most Effective to Least Effective – Boys vs Girls

Boys Top 10 Challenges	Ranking	Girls Top 10 Challenges
Be in Nature	1	Be in Nature
Choose Your Own	2	Gratitude
Unplug Before Sleeping	3	Choose Your Own
Aerobic Exercise	4	How Others See Me
Make Bed & Tidy Up	5	Decluttering
Gratitude	6	Aerobic Exercise
Air Boxing	7	Unplug Before Sleeping
Hold a Plank	8	Deep Breathing
How Others See Me	9	Guided Meditation
Act of Kindness	10	Create Joy List

Challenges Ranked in Order of Most Effective to Least Effective - Family Placement

Oldest Children	Middle Children	Youngest Children	Only Children
Be in Nature	Be in Nature	Be in Nature	Be in Nature
Guided Meditation	Decluttering	How Others See Me	Choose Your Own
Aerobic Exercise	How Others See me	Decluttering	Gratitude
Choose Your Own	Choose Your Own	Choose Your Own	How Others See Me
Gratitude	Unplug Before Sleeping	Aerobic Exercise	Unplug Before Sleeping

Challenges Ranked in Order of Most Effective to Least Effective - Grade Level

Freshmen (9th gr.)	Sophomore (10th gr.)	Junior (11th gr.)	Senior (12th gr.)
Conversation Starters	Unplug Before Sleeping	Be in Nature	Be in Nature
Air Boxing	Stretching Yoga	Choose Your Own	Guided Meditation
Gratitude	Make Bed & Tidy Up	How Others See Me	Choose Your Own
Act of Kindness	How Others See Me	Decluttering	Deep Breathing
Guided Meditation	Hold a Plank	Unplug Before Sleeping	Compliment Someone

CHAPTER 5

The Findings

We were anticipating some changes to the students' mental health and wellness as a result of the IMPACT Project, and we were hopeful the overall changes would be positive. After the completion of the research portion, we were blown away with the level of transformation the students experienced, and the sheer number of ways they saw shifts. For a comprehensive exploration into the Findings, please refer to Chapter 19, Deeper Insights into the Findings. Below are the biggest takeaways:

1. Growth-mindset plays a big role in determining the outcome.
2. Resilience and perseverance can be developed through intentional practice.
3. Mindfulness matters in stress-management.
4. Physical activity was effective, and the kind of activity brought different results.
5. Students crave connection and friendship with like-minded people.
6. When they had the choice for a challenge topic, they followed their desires.
7. Family placement did play a role in the strategies the students preferred.
8. Grade trends showed significant growth in self-awareness and self-care.

9. Gender revealed patterns and preferences in the four categories of challenges.
10. The entrenched habits around phones were revealed, as was the freedom of unplugging.
11. Leadership is not reserved for the few; they all confidently found the leader in themselves.

The Finding that Summed It All Up

As an educator, it's heartbreaking to see your student struggle and experience such sadness, frustration, and disengagement because of stress and overwhelm. We knew we would be sharing powerful strategies for mental health support throughout the five month experience, so before we welcomed the students into week one, we designed various ways to measure the state of their mind and their outlook before and after the project.

In our pre-assessment, we asked our students to explain how they were feeling, what they were experiencing, and their general outlook on their academics, friendships, and their future. Their most frequently used words are represented in the first word cloud below. Their words give us insight into the level of their frustration, worry, anxiety, fear, and overwhelm.

In our post-assessment questionnaire, we asked the same questions about how they were feeling, what they were experiencing, and their general outlook on their academics, friendships, and their future. The words they used are displayed in the second word cloud below. This simple brainstorming list became the finding that truly summed up the full impact of the project. We can see their transformation by the words they used and the positivity they shared.

How The Students Described Their Feelings Prior to the IMPACT Project

Struggle
Judgement Overwhelmed
conflict
Worried Tired
Pressure Stressed Sucks
Scream Exhausted Unmanageable
Rejection Breakdown
Cry grades Hard
Procrastination
Frustrated
exams Disorganized Anxious
Upset Insecure
Overscheduled

How The Students Described Their Feelings After the IMPACT Project

growth-mindset positive
appreciate mindful optimistic
connection
accomplished joy successful
determination calmer
happier grit believe leader
accepting goals peace
strong motivated
balance gratitude organized
achievement
focused confident

CHAPTER 6

The Benefits

Through this project, we wanted to equip our students with the knowledge and practice of various strategies to support their mental health and reduce their stress and struggle. However, with a comprehensive program like this, there were bound to be other benefits besides learning new skills. Below we outline some of the major benefits the students experienced as a result of our time together, normalizing mental health issues, holding open discussions, and sharing our experiences so we could all learn and grow.

For each benefit below, we share a quote from one of our teen authors to illustrate how they experienced growth, development, skill acquisition, or confidence.

Growth Mindset	I was personally not comfortable with reaching out and starting a conversation, so this week's challenge was very difficult. However, I decided to try, and I managed to do the activity by following the given directions, and it turned out successfully.
Boost Resilience	I would say before the IMPACT Project I would let stress of schoolwork and life really drag me down, but after the program, I can release and handle that stress in a healthier way. I now have strategies and the challenges we did to help me overcome my stress, and not let stress of school and things like that ruin my day.
Reduce Overwhelm	I was extremely overwhelmed with homework, AP tests, sports, and so much more. I didn't have a steady coping mechanism which made the pressure even worse. I always felt like I wasn't doing enough, and I never felt fully satisfied with anything I did. Now, I'm implementing these challenges into my life, and it has really helped me reduce my overwhelm, and feel less anxious and stressed.
Manage Anxiety	I'm so grateful to finally be able to know more about myself and my emotions. By building better self-awareness, I know what strategies will work to calm myself down and help me when I'm feeling very anxious.
Improve Concentration	Doing some of the challenges helped me with my homework because I had more focus and better recall of material, so it seemed easier and faster.
Better Time Management	My time managing skills got much better after this project because of the challenges and trainings. I often had to give up things I wanted to do because I couldn't manage my time. Now I get everything done and have time to relax and be with my friends, which improved my connection with others and lifted my confidence.
Persevere	I now know that I can overcome any difficulties or challenges, as long as I am determined to persevere to overcome them. Also, I now know I can learn and keep growing from my mistakes.
Improve Relationships	I was able to learn a lot about my friend's childhood, which was really interesting and turned out great. With another friend, I ended up having a really deep conversation about "success" in life. It helped me create stronger bonds with my friends.

Help Others	Helping my friend actually made my day. It was like a "Give and Take". You give them compliments of what they have or what they wear. And you receive this "magic" called happiness from somewhere. It would make me smile and think that giving compliments is really giving yourself happiness.
Better Sleep	Now I fall asleep quicker and sleep more peacefully at night. My mind is clearer, and it isn't racing with things I have to do the next morning. I am sleeping better and having more dreams. I don't wake up feeling drained and tired like before.
Get Active	I think exercising was mentally and physically good. In terms of its physical effects, exercising and getting your heart pumping is beneficial to your body, and releases endorphins. Mentally, it let me focus on something else and get away from my problems temporarily, providing a nice change.
Be Grateful	Before I created my gratitude lists, I was feeling very lost. As I wrote my lists, I realized I had taken some things for granted, and I saw how blessed I am with everything that I have, and I became more thankful. I am lucky to be alive.
Feel Hopeful	I feel a lot more confident about my future, and that I will be able to find a way to succeed.
Enjoy Nature	Being in nature impacted me mentally and emotionally because it relieved me from my pain and overwhelm and helped me to relax. I reflected on positive things in my past, and felt my stress and problems fade away. Nature's extraordinary scenery left me in awe.
Notice the Small Things	Many of the challenges were small, and at first the changes made weren't noticeable. As time passed though, I started to see that the small changes over time became really impactful.

Part III
Teens Talk

CHAPTER 7

What is One Quality You Admire About Me?

By Lindsey Hyewon Lee

Tears.

Tears streaming down my face like Niagara Falls. Nose clogged with snot. Cheeks flushed red. Watery, red eyes like an angry chihuahua with a mean allergy. But these were not sad tears; they were tears of joy. And it was all because of one simple question: *What's one quality that you admire about me?*

When we compliment one another, we often use the common responses of *nice* and *kind*. These are valid compliments; after all, who doesn't want to be called nice and kind? But when we consider how often we default to these words, the value of them is reduced. It becomes redundant. *Nice* becomes a casual answer that serves as a template for complimenting all people. By relying on this description, it is difficult to see a person's intrinsic value because *nice* strips them of their *specialness*.

As I passed through life only hearing the same generic descriptors, I felt like your Average Joe. I felt like I was worth nothing more than my value for being "nice" to others. *Why can't anyone think of anything else great about me? Is that all I am? "Nice?"* These were the thoughts and questions that plagued my mind prior to entering this project.

When I started this weekly challenge, I entered with the expectation that I would hear this generic response. It began with a simple text on Instagram. I asked one good friend, "What's one quality that you admire about me?" As I eagerly awaited their response, thumping inside of me was my anxiety over the fear that my question was too direct, too out of the blue.

To my surprise, my friend responded with sincerity thirty minutes later. I didn't see the words *nice* or *kind*. Instead, I saw a block of text that gushed with their genuine raw feelings and thoughts. They called me "sensitive and bold." So long *nice* Joe, and hello *sensitive and bold* Joe. I was stunned by their openness and thoughtfulness. It moved me precisely because it starkly contrasted with the way I had viewed myself. They didn't just put in a few descriptive words; I could feel the thought put into their reply as they elaborated on their *why*. They took it as an opportunity to share their true thoughts of me, and the authenticity touched my heart.

As a reserved person who finds that socializing doesn't come as easily as others, many people often comment on what I would consider to be my outer shell, saying I seem distant and timid. I can see that. I'm not a social butterfly, and I prefer to spend my time in quieter spaces when I need to recharge my social battery. However, I also love talking to and being with people and I am a very warm person who cares deeply about others. To see that my friend noticed my hidden true attribute touched me to the bottom of my heart. I felt she saw my essence, who I truly was, and it was enlivening.

Her words filled me with so much emotion– I immediately called her. As I wiped the tears from my eyes, I shared qualities about what I admired in her, reciprocating her genuineness. We shared a tearful and emotional conversation peeking behind the masks we present to society, and it was magical. That's when I felt the true power of the IMPACT Project.

What I hope to share with you is that people are truly unexpected. Sometimes, we are so occupied by our own thoughts and expectations that we build a tall, intimidating wall that prevents social interactions.

We hide behind it, blocking off the niceties of *nice* and *kind*, shielding ourselves in fear of revealing an inch of our true, bare selves. We want to be seen, but vulnerability is simply scary. When we build that wall, even with the intention of keeping away negativity, we also prevent positive interactions from happening, and we hide away our quirks that make us unique. Keep in mind that YOU are building that wall. YOU have the power to begin the process of breaking down your walls. YOU can step beyond your paradigm of fear and approach the world with a lens of optimism and hope. Our experiences may not be entirely the same, but I hope you reimagine your own identity by taking a step in the deeper end and reflecting with others.

Making My Bed Helped Me in Ways I Didn't Imagine

Rrrrrrrring.
Rrrrrrrrrrrrrrrring.
RRRRRRRRRRINNNNNNG.

Another wonderful morning. I peek at my phone to turn off the alarm, only for my finger to *accidentally* slip on the snooze button for another 5 minutes of shut-eye. Five minutes later, another peek and another *accident* occurs. As I come to accept that one too many accidents are intentional, I hastily jump out of bed to prepare myself for school. My beloved stuffed bear, sweet, little Blueberry, flung out of bed with me, landing on the floor. My blankets poked out of the crevices of the railings of my loft bed. My bed sheets were left as a wrinkled mess, and it appeared that Godzilla had left his nest. The chaos reminded me that our challenge this week was to make our beds in the morning.

Before I did anything else, I tackled my bed. I neatly unraveled the tangled sheets from the mattress, rearranged Blueberry and her little stuffed animal friends in straight rows so they lined up like a forest of fluff, patted my pillow well for giving me a good night's rest, and used my hand as an iron to flatten out the blanket. I stood back and admired my work. My bed was Pinterest-worthy, and I smiled. The years of nagging and pleading from my mother to make my bed came to mind, and it made sense. It was a simple task, and it made me feel accomplished first thing in the morning.

It seems like an exaggeration, but the impact this little act made was profound; it left its mark in my mind and body. Every day, I woke up with a clear objective: make my bed. I had always had other tasks to do in the morning, like brush my teeth and get to school on time, but this one was more tangible. I loved walking into my room at the end of a long or hard day, and being welcomed by my perfect, cozy bed. Within a few days of starting this challenge, I found myself feeling more accomplished because I carried the success from my morning all day long.

One day, feeling particularly crushed by a barrage of daunting assignments, formidable projects, and a colossal level of exams and quizzes, I was ragged from fatigue. However, when I got to my room, my perfect little bed was waiting for me. I climbed up onto the loft, slid between the cold sheets, and cuddled sweet little Blueberry close to my heart for a tight snuggle as I waited for my blankets to warm me up. I was able to let go of the stress from my day, and I felt content. With the perfectly fluffed pillow that held my head and neck, and the blanket as soft as a cloud weighing evenly down on my body with great warmth, the experience of sleep was never better. I felt like a champion welcomed back after a grueling fight.

This challenge had two parts. The first was making our bed every morning, and the second was tidying up our rooms every night. As the sun set behind the horizon, I would start putting things away before going to sleep. It was as simple as returning my notebook to my schoolbag, putting away my stationary, and wiping away the dust on my desk.

I noticed that there was a significant difference concerning the condition of my desk from before and after the challenge. Before, I often left my workspace in chaos, as if a tornado had passed through. But then, I realized I was the tornado, and this challenge showed me I was also the first responder who would help after the disaster. As I prepared myself for the emergency, I grabbed my green duster and my trusty vacuum cleaner and jumped in. Each night, I put every little displaced object back in its place and dusted the surfaces around my room. I reunited old lovers that were parted by the table and floor, neatly folded together to return to their home–the sock drawer. I rescued a dainty little pencil from the dark depths behind my desk. I found ancient written artifacts from school that had gotten lost under the mountain of books and papers that had been taking over my workspace. Cleaning had effects beyond the clearing of the physical space; cleaning became a metaphor for cleansing my mind. When I was organizing my room, I was also organizing my thoughts.

Despite the benefits, these two tasks weren't easy habits to form. It can feel tedious to make your bed or tidy up your desk when you are tired, busy, and having long days. However, the rewards are worth it. This challenge will only take a sliver of your time, yet it has the potential to make your day or make your night. Something GREAT and AMAZING can happen from even the smallest of actions. I continue to practice making my bed in the morning now, recalling not only my mother's voice in my head, but also my own words of encouragement knowing that this small little thing makes me feel good all day long.

When Decluttering Hurts So Good

Piles of unworn clothes, plushies from dear childhood, ragged baby blankets, ancient little trinkets lying in the corner, pieces of yarn I kept in promise of learning how to knit... these are the items that are littered throughout my room like precious little treasures. I scavenged through my closet wondering if I would find any "new" clothes that I had never known were mine, and I felt like I entered a forest of clothing. I took out a dress that I had loved for many years and smiled. It was a lovely, pale yellow, floral dress with thin straps and a skirt that flared like a spring flower. I held onto it for so long with the expectation that I would be able to fit into it. With a heart heavy with fear, I held it up to my body; I noticed that my body barely matched the width of the dress. I was devastated. Guilt swept over me, followed by the promise to diet, to lose weight, and to shape my body to fit societal standards. I could not embrace my body for what it was, I could only see what it was not. I had tried to break the toxic cycle that had continued for months, yet this little, itty bitty dress from the depths of my closet flooded me with pain and shame all over again.

In my mind, I heard all the voices of criticism that people hear about their bodies.

"You are too fat."

"You are too skinny."

"You are too feminine."

"You are too masculine."

"You are too ugly. Get plastic surgery."

With the Decluttering Challenge, I gained the courage to say enough was enough. I broke the shackles of *what ifs* and *unachievable* standards in society, setting myself free. I grabbed the pale yellow dress and threw it into the bin that would soon hold a compilation of old trinkets and unwanted items from my room.

Once I had discarded the flowery little beast, I realized I truly had vanquished the villain from my heart. I cut the pale yellow threads that suffocated me, and for the first time, I could breathe deeply and see my true value. I felt it in my heart. I really did it. I conquered that villain. I was no longer the person that would remain in agony over the perception of my body. I was now someone who could begin the process of reconciling with my body, apologizing for ever doubting its beauty and perfection for functioning and living. My body was immaculate as it was; the dress had to shape to *my* body. The past, the expectations, the pressure, all would eventually be wiped away with my efforts to cleanse my surroundings. Because in the end, these memories and feelings would only truly resurface by the ideological embodiments of the objects I carried. The dainty yellow dress that bloomed like a flower was muddled with stains of my shame, guilt, and inability to adhere to societal body standards. Getting rid of the physical object purged the negativity from my mind of itself.

But we have to be real. It's hard to get rid of things, to declutter. Sometimes we latch on because of old memories and feelings of hope that the items possess. Sometimes we cling to them because we think it's all we deserve. Even though deciding to get rid of those items was the first step, we don't always move forward;

sometimes we take a few steps back. As I kept cleaning out my room, I found myself wanting to revisit that little dress. I still loved its soft fabric and delicate flowers. It was a beautiful dress. However, behind those thoughts in my head, I could see that judgment and shame still existed and I knew I was better off without the dress in my life. The dress represented too many things: the expectation to be pretty, the expectation to be feminine, the expectation to be perfect. The dress was a constant reminder of my inability to accept my imperfections. With it finally gone, I could put my mind at peace. It was okay if I didn't fit into the dress. I am beautiful without the dress.

It takes time to truly let go of the memories that are carried within our items. However, you can't hold onto the past forever. And sometimes, it's a barrier that prevents you from moving forward. We need to make room for new memories and objects precisely because we cannot hold all pieces of our history until the end of time. Life is so unexpected. There are so many great things that it offers for everyone. Although we can't choose when or what we receive, we can certainly control how we prepare ourselves for those new opportunities. Some burdens of the past can weigh us down more than others, thus it is critical to keep ourselves light enough to march forward into the future ahead of us. It doesn't have to be a sad process; removing remnants of the past can act as a passage to facilitate your own very growth as an individual. It can be empowering and liberating. It's all about choosing to release parts of your past that you no longer see as beneficial for you. That old little shirt that you've kept in your closet for so long can transition you to the new phase of your life once you let go of it. It's hard, but extremely necessary.

When Joy is Hard, Choose Gratitude

Slam!

I shut my laptop and pushed myself away from my desk to rest my eyes for a moment. I dimmed my desk lights, switched on some of my most favorite piano pieces, grabbed my fuzzy blanket and wrapped it around myself as if I was a newborn being swaddled. But like little dust particles, the undone tasks on my to-do list floated all around me. I decided to start working on this week's challenge: creating a Joy List of all the things we loved. I was hopeful it would relieve some of my stress and anxiety. I thought it could be a scrapbook of memories and loved ones. In theory, it was supposed to make me happy. But it didn't make me FEEL happy, at least not in the way I hoped it would. Rather than making me feel good, it only made me more frustrated. I sat on my chair, my mind contemplating what I thought would bring me joy. Seconds, minutes, and hours would pass by as my mind feverishly cycled through memories and experiences in hopes to find something. Nothing came to mind. Instead of making me feel better, this challenge left me anxious, stressed, and frustrated that I couldn't get it done. Why couldn't I think of anything happy? I abandoned my Joy List with a feeling of despair.

A few weeks later, we had a new challenge. I was busy most of the night working on projects for school and chores around my house. As the evening grew darker and the chirping of the crickets filled the night air, I started the Gratitude Challenge. I sat on my living room couch, placed my laptop on a cushion over my lap for extra coziness, and powered on my round little speaker.

After struggling with my Joy List Challenge earlier in the program, I didn't expect much this time. I thought to myself, "How different could a gratitude list be from a joy list?" I closed my eyes, listened to the soft ambiance of some Billie Eilish, and allowed my mind to ponder, *what am I grateful for?* Little ideas and happy thoughts and fun experiences illuminated my mind, showing me so many things that I was grateful for in my life. I created a long, exhaustive list of items of gratitude, and every day in the weekly challenge, I looked back on all my entries and added some more items that drew a smile on my face. I had so many things to be grateful for in so many parts of my life. I felt my heart feeling lighter as if it was on clouds every moment I looked back. It piqued happiness in my heart, but deep inside of me, I also began to wonder, why did the Joy List Challenge not work for me?

Perhaps it was the Billie Eilish song, but on further reflection, I realized it was the circumstances. With the Joy List Challenge, school pressure and demands were at an all-time high. I was consumed with stress; I was frantically completing projects left and right, assignments up and down, and studying for tests that fell onto me from all directions. My mind was clogged with academic facts and figures and formulas, there was no mental space to sit and think about what had made me feel happy.

And the truth was, I didn't even know what made me happy. From a young age, we are told to be happy, but it's an abstract idea. We don't know what happiness truly is or how to find it. We're never taught how to be happy, then when we are older, we never have the time to find out because of the sheer amount of work, school, and society places on us. That is the critical issue that impacted me tremendously: not only was I stressed out of my mind with all my commitments and course work, I had to define and discover happiness as a concept, which is hard to understand even when you are happy.

However, with the Gratitude Challenge, I would realize it was all about the circumstances. I was in a place of adequacy in my life; I was not particularly happy or sad, just in the middle. Some might even say it was a boring time. I wasn't as busy as I was before, and there wasn't anything necessarily exciting happening in my life. With no projects being slammed on my face or exciting games emerging in my peripheral, life just felt a little spacious. It felt wonderful. As I set the mood with music, comfort food, pillows, and blankets, I found myself capable of exploring the depths of my heart to reach that core feeling of gratitude. I didn't have to think about the larger philosophy behind the concept of happiness or the feelings of joy that my experiences brought me. With gratitude as a framework, I could think of anything that simply existed in my life.

I'm grateful for my family.
I'm grateful for my blanket.
I'm grateful for Billie Eilish.

Throughout the week as the stress piled up, I found that the previous entries I had made in my journal had lightened up my mood and opened a pathway in my mind for the stress to be released. I would giggle to myself as I saw my entry, "I am grateful for dumplings," or "I am grateful for Korean dramas." When I had the emotional and mental leisure to stretch my mind and reflect thoughtfully, my gratitude list had become a list of reminders of what I loved. My Joy List.

When I think about the Joy List Challenge and the Gratitude Challenge, they were actually quite similar. However, the difference was timing. During a really stressful time in my life, creating a Joy List was not easy, useful, or possible because I didn't have the mental capacity to do it. My brain was buzzing with writing essays, brainstorming experimental designs, and solving complex math problems; I didn't even know where to begin. I couldn't bother to add one more thing to my checklist or put another question in my head.

In contrast, when I had the leisure, the time, and the privilege of having a moment of quiet, creating a gratitude list helped me note down and appreciate the beauty of the life I lived.

So, the Joy List Challenge wasn't the best fit for me at that moment. And you know what? That's okay. Not all challenges work for everyone. Even if I didn't feel any happier after, I found value in learning about timing, and now that the school year ended, I could slowly start answering that question: what is *my* happiness? I could begin defining my own happiness from now on. I would take the initiative of pulling happiness into me; I would chase for happiness no more.

Sometimes your expectations don't align with your reality, and that is the importance of trying new things. You just never know until you try it. I never knew that gratitude journaling could have such a positive impact on me despite the roadblock I had hit with creating a joy list. That's why it's important to revisit and understand why something did or didn't work for you. Experimenting with challenges can help you to understand yourself, and by understanding yourself, you can foster your confidence in carrying yourself as the unique being you are. Gratitude comes from a genuine place of the heart, and when we have a grateful heart, we may find joy lives there too.

An Interview With Author Lindsey Hyewon Lee

Why did you join the IMPACT Project?

School. Extracurriculars. Homework. A constant cycle of rushing to school in the morning, attending class, and returning home for more work. At times, life can feel repetitive and circular. Although these activities were exhilarating, ultimately, it was exhausting. The IMPACT Project gave me time to focus on my self-growth, learning from my experiences to achieve my greatest potential. I hoped to find an opportunity to truly blossom as an individual, and through the experiences it offered, I found room for passion in my heart.

Your stories showed us some really memorable moments about building resilience and gaining confidence, but I can imagine that some challenges transformed you but weren't your favorite ones. What were your favorite challenges?

1. Decluttering
2. Deep Breathing
3. Complimenting Someone

How would you describe yourself before and after the IMPACT Project? What are the biggest changes you notice about yourself?

The IMPACT Project changed me in ways that mattered to me. I have transformed into a mindset of improvement that can no longer tolerate the stagnation of life that I had dreaded prior. With the weekly challenges, I have grown confident in the power I wield to make change in my life. I am my greatest enemy, but I am also my greatest ally. Before, I felt hesitant to try such new things because it was *different*, but now by pushing myself out of my comfort zone, I feel empowered to take action to become a better person to both my peers and for myself. There is always room for improvement, and my experience here has only motivated me to strive for that greater ideal.

What advice would you give those who feel stressed, stuck, under pressure, or overwhelmed and don't know what to do?

When you feel stuck, do something! Take action. If you're stuck on what type of action to take, here's one thing I immediately recommend you do: go outside, take a walk in nature and remove yourself from your usual daily space. Inhale the fresh, crisp air by surrounding yourself with greens of all kinds. Allow yourself to feel the grass, smell the grass, and hear the grass. I like lying down in the grass, taking in all the breezes that I encounter to be present in the moment. It gives you an opportunity to place yourself out of your routine of business and keep yourself occupied. Nature is incredibly beautiful and powerful in so many ways, perhaps all you need to take a push forward from the rut you experience is but a small break. Just like it helped me, I hope it helps you.

Do you have any final words of wisdom?

Self-discovery is a process. Take initiative to immerse yourself in the experiences around you and peek into your preferences.

About the Author

Lindsey Hyewon Lee

Lindsey Lee is an aspiring Korean-American author who hopes to incorporate her skills in writing with her burning passion for biology to pursue a career in healthcare. She is eager to dissect the emotional health and well-being of adolescents to learn more about how to help her community peers. Born and raised in California, she faced unique struggles in her childhood when her family moved to South Korea for four years. Lindsey joined the IMPACT Project as co-president with hopes of sharing her experiences with her peers to foster and lead a community of distinct perspectives to learn from.

As a rising high school senior, she spends much of her time outside of the classroom participating in policy debate, volunteering with the American Red Cross, advocating for social causes, and involving herself in local organizations like Koreatown Youth + Community Center (KYCC). Beyond her love for giving back to her community, Lindsey has an unhealthy obsession with strawberries that she equips to fuel her daily endeavors. You will most likely find her at Starbucks writing away or wandering in the middle of nature looking for a warm place to nap.

CHAPTER 8

The Best Competitor is Not Who You Think

By Brian Son

I was on the hard ground to do my first plank of the week. I set up my phone timer and got into position. I started to moan and grunt, and it was much harder than I expected. I looked at my timer, thinking I would reach sixty seconds easily, but I had just passed the thirty second mark.

'Uh, oh, this is not what I expected.'

I tasted something salty in my mouth, and it was my SWEAT! Oh, gross! I wanted to give up and set a lower goal for tomorrow, but I tried my best and held on for as long as possible.

Right after my timer passed fifty seconds, I lost my mind and collapsed on the floor. I could feel the sweat on my back and even though it was very unpleasant and uncomfortable, I realized something; I didn't really hate that. If I am honest, it actually felt pretty good. All the sweats and grunts I expressed were evidence of my hard work. I was kind of excited for the next day's plank because I looked forward to how much more I could endure tomorrow. I had no doubt that I would do better.

The next day, I came back to the hard, cold floor ready to do my second plank. I now had a new thought in my head that 'if I fall down earlier or at the same time as yesterday, it means I lost to myself and I didn't grow.' I know this thinking is not a good way to get motivated and stay inspired, but it helped me a lot to endure the discomfort. I was surprised that after I finished thinking about my motto, the timer passed 40 seconds already!

Right away, I got very tired, and I felt something itchy on my head. And along with the sticky sweat forming on my forehead, I felt my head and entire body getting hotter and hotter from the exercise. My face was getting red, and as I felt the temperature rising, I knew I was done for today. I immediately checked my timer: fifty-six seconds. I was so close to the one minute goal I had on the first day.

Seeing my seconds increase each day was so motivating. I continued the same routine every day, and with every groan I increased my plank by a few seconds until I hit my personal best of 67 seconds by the last day of the challenge. When I thought I could hold a plank for sixty seconds, I had no idea what it would be like. However, after working on it all week, I made it higher than my initial goal and I was very proud of myself. I believe that my desire to win against myself by performing better than the previous day made this result possible.

Throughout this experience, I learned something important. If you asked me in the past whether competing against someone, including myself, is good or bad, I would definitely answer that competing is a negative way of learning and growing. Competing against someone always results in a winner and a loser.

However, I realized that 'competing' is not always a bad thing because competing is a form of challenging ourselves to become better. This exercise taught me that I could compete with myself to strive for bigger and better results. Sometimes that is through hardships, and sometimes that is through challenges so big we don't know if we will prevail. However, when we set a goal to strive for, and focus on it with everything we've got, we can build the confidence to do things we never thought we could achieve.

Mindset First, Then Change Follows

Zzz...Zzz...My alarm woke me up at 7:25am. I rubbed my eyes and turned it off because the noise was annoying. Then as I was lying in my bed, I remembered this week's challenge was to make my bed. When I first got information about the challenge, I secretly questioned the purpose of this exercise. Then Angela and Leanne showed us a video called, "Make Your Bed," by Admiral William H. McRaven in his commencement speech to the graduating class of the University of Texas at Austin in 2014. He said, "if you want to change the world, make your bed." Then I thought, *'That doesn't make sense! What's the point? I don't know of any reason to do it.'*

On the first day, I didn't want to do it but I did it anyways because it was our challenge. I held the edges of my blanket and tossed it over my bed. I put my pillows back to their original spot. There. I'm done, right? I was feeling annoyed by this challenge; I didn't want to do it just because someone told me to do it.

But on the second day and third day, something started to change in my mindset, and I decided to try this challenge with a better frame of mind. I realized that making my bed didn't take much effort, and it wasn't really that annoying because it was pretty quick and easy. I'm honestly not sure why I didn't want to do it. I could clearly notice the change of mood as the days went by. For example, I focused on the annoyance of the challenge in the beginning, however, my perspective toward the challenge gradually became more positive.

Something else I noticed was how it impacted my mood. I felt better seeing my bed made nicely after coming home from a really crappy day. And, when I made my bed first thing in the morning, I started my day with something I had already done well. So even when I spent hours overthinking my math test grade, or how I had to finish three science labs, or how I had to prepare for an upcoming essay, I had already accomplished something good each day before I left my room.

After a week of making my bed, the words from that admiral started to make more sense. Success comes from small achievements. I felt proud and accomplished after making my bed every morning, but it wasn't just about my bed; I felt it in other parts of my life too. My worries about school and negative thoughts still existed, but they didn't bother me as much anymore. I was confident to take on all the other tasks on my list, and my feeling of accomplishment grew stronger because I created a momentum of achievement.

This challenge was the beginning of creating a new and useful habit for my future. If you make your bed every morning, you will feel accomplished and be proud of the small task that you completed. By starting your day with a positive feeling, you can also end the day with pride. Everything starts from a little tiny step.

Kindness is Contagious

Once again, I saw my tennis coach struggling with our team because nobody wanted to stay after practice and pick up the dozens of remaining balls on the ground. Because of this, he had to choose different people every day. I clearly saw the frowns on their faces, and I could see they wanted to complain, but couldn't.

For this week's challenge, we were to complete random acts of kindness for others. I decided to volunteer to help my coach after practice pick up the tennis balls that week. Even though it was such a hot and humid day, I picked up the balls with sweat dripping down my back.

As I was helping my coach, I also enjoyed the fact that I got a chance to spend more time with him than usual. I realized that by showing an act of kindness to someone, I get an opportunity to build a better relationship with them. He thanked me a lot for volunteering, instead of being "voluntold." His praise lifted my mood and motivated me to work harder and help him even more.

I really enjoyed helping at tennis, and I kept my eye open for other opportunities.

On another day, one of the school's jazz band members asked for volunteers to help organize the seating and the sound system for the jazz concert that was happening soon. I didn't think I would have time since I was playing the drum set in the concert and I was busy preparing for my own piece. However, no one volunteered at first. I saw him struggling to set up the concert all by himself, so I offered to help him. Then surprisingly, others joined in to help too.

Even though these were two different experiences, they had something in common. In the beginning, both my tennis teammates and the other band members didn't really want to help because it made them go out of their way. However, when I stepped up to show an act of kindness, other people noticed my actions, and decided to help too. I realized that I can be the one to spread a positive impact to my community by helping others because acts of kindness can actually be contagious.

By committing to this challenge for a week, I gradually started to see more acts of kindness happening around me that I didn't notice before. Adults taking care of children, friends complimenting other friends, people spending time with elders, and teens donating to organizations; I was happy to observe that all these people engaging in different acts of kindness can inspire more people to do more acts of kindness and spread goodness in the world.

Moving Mountains One Can at a Time

Four Coke cans, two plastic water bottles from Costco, three sunglasses, an ice pack, a bunch of snack wrappers, pens, chargers, nail clippers, a Rubik's cube... all crammed onto my desk. I remember the good old days before COVID when my desk used to be spotless, when I could actually see every single inch of the grainy wood surface. For the last two years, however, I just kept piling on more and more stuff.

COVID changed me; I got lazy, stopped caring about anything, gave up in a lot of ways, and lost my motivation to do things that I had easily done before. My surroundings became messy, and I became even messier.

For this week's challenge, we were assigned to declutter our rooms. At first, I didn't see the importance of this challenge and I believed that it was unnecessary. Things were fine, weren't they? I had become so used to living in my messy and unorganized environment for such a long time, I didn't even remember my tidy and ordered life before COVID. This Decluttering challenge felt like a chore.

For the first few days, I started with cleaning my desk because that seemed to be the easiest. After the third day of decluttering my desk, I felt organized and happy about my cleaner room. However, that happiness didn't last because the next day when I opened my closet to choose my clothes, I saw a stack of t-shirts from years ago that were too small. I had more decluttering to do.

Sometimes I hear people talking about how they don't want to get rid of things because they might want or need them again someday. For me, I didn't hesitate to throw my clothes away because I knew I wouldn't wear them anymore; I was ready to move on. I abruptly grabbed a white trash bag and ruthlessly started throwing away my shirts, one by one. I didn't see it as a loss, instead I felt refreshed and organized when I was done.

I looked at all that I had decluttered that week and I felt very proud and happy. My desk was now ordered, neat, and clean, and my closet was organized and ready to store new clothes I wanted to buy. Also, by decluttering my room for an entire week, I started to build a habit of cleaning out things before they become a mountain in my way.

And I realized something more important: little things matter. Cleaning my room and organizing my desk was the start of me becoming a better person. Because I had my surroundings organized and cleared, my thoughts also became organized and calm. When I spend a short amount of time decluttering my mess, it actually brought up a huge amount of change. I felt better, my mind was clearer to do homework, and felt more motivated to do more things.

Big things always begin from small things, and that is why little things matter. Throughout the week, I learned that having a clean outside environment makes me a more peaceful and confident person. Whenever I'm overwhelmed, I now know how to "un-overwhelm" myself because external order creates internal calm.

An Interview With Author Brian Son

Why did you join the IMPACT Project?

In the beginning of the project, I thought it would be fun to be in a challenge-based project with other like-minded people. Now, after meeting these great people, I eagerly want to see what the project members and I can achieve with our new skills and abilities. I definitely saw some changes in myself after experiencing the project, and I think I will continue to change over time, especially in areas of personal growth and leadership. Especially after this experience, I believe these two areas are the most important pieces to becoming a successful person in society. Knowing what you did wrong, fixing it, and changing yourself is how you become a better person.

Your stories showed us some really memorable moments about building resilience and gaining confidence, but I can imagine that some challenges transformed you but weren't your favorite ones. What would you say were your favorite challenges to do?

1. Conversation Starter
2. Compliment Someone
3. How Others See Me

Over the course of the program, I am sure you changed in many ways. What do you now know about your ability to overcome hard things?

I stay positive as long as possible to maintain my mental health and feelings. I now know how to get help from trusted adults and friends when I am stuck. The IMPACT Project was definitely the biggest factor in making all these changes in me. The various weekly challenges helped a lot by providing multiple opportunities to communicate with trusted adults and friends. Every time we had the weekly meeting with our group, I learned new ways to solve my problems because of the discussions and training sessions. From there I learned that personal growth and leadership can be improved more by interacting with other people and learning from others, which I didn't know before.

What advice would you give those who feel stressed, stuck, under pressure, or overwhelmed and don't know what to do?

Always remember that your effort and enthusiasm will eventually pay you back in the end; therefore you should stay positive and bright even when you are stuck because I know it will be worse if you get depressed and lack power or energy. Also, don't beat yourself up, either physically and verbally, because you are a better person than that, and try not to blame others as well. We have to find a way to be successful for everyone involved in the situation, where everyone can be happy.

Do you have any final words of wisdom?

Don't give up. All the work you've done, every effort you've put in, and every minute you've spent will eventually compensate you at some point.

About the Author

Brian Son

That one boy who attracts the hearts of others, Brian Son is an author who pictures his life as one big journey. Brian moved to the U.S. during 5th grade, and he is now a rising junior in high school in Irvine, California. He is a mindful, understanding, and helpful person who is compassionate with many different kinds of people. Brian started falling in love with mental health from the day he realized that he is fascinated with people's thoughts and feelings.

Brian is on the tennis team at his school, and enjoys practicing tennis during his free time. He often coaches youth and teenagers with their skills when he does not have any practice.

Brian was a co-president during the IMPACT Project and shared many insights in the group discussions. He tries his best to be responsible and mature at all times to be a role model for others. He sees how powerful it is to spread positive encouragement to others who are in a similar situation as him, or those who are struggling in their life. In college, he wants to major in communications and continue to graduate school for an MBA. He would love to work in a business that can help and serve many different people.

CHAPTER 9

The Most Unexpected Gift

By Chloe Sy-Perez

It was 9 p.m. and I still hadn't asked someone about something they admired about me. I walked into the kitchen and noticed my mom at the counter mindlessly scrolling through her phone. Her droopy eyes and long face told me that she had a tiresome day and sleep will find her soon. I quietly drifted next to her and poked her softly.

"Mom," I started to say, "I have to do this challenge and it's really awkward. I need to ask someone to name one thing they admire about me. I was wondering if you could help me? You don't have to say a lot, just one thing will do."

She stopped looking at her phone and faced me. "One thing? But what if I have so many?"

My mom and I have a great relationship. When we're frustrated, we speak our hearts out to each other. If I need encouragement, I can always count on her to keep me going. If she needs someone's advice on a decision, I'm always there for her. But talking about the things we love about each other isn't our strong suit. We believe our actions toward each other speak louder than words. Sometimes all it takes is cleaning the house for her to know that I love her and want to make her day easier.

"Chloe... I have watched you grow up, fall down, get back up, and overcome the hardest moments in your life. Remember that time in your freshman year when you started to get really sick? You still went to your 6 a.m. cross country practice and when your coach noticed something was wrong, he told you to call me. Then you still wanted to go to your first period and take your Biology test. That day we found out you got shingles, but that didn't stop you from emailing your teachers, studying for every test you had to miss, and finishing all your assignments. Although you can be stubborn, your resilience always pushes you through and I admire that about you. You don't let the little things bring you down. If there's a problem, I can always count on your creativity to fix it. Like that time in elementary when your teacher ran out of plates to pass beans around for the art project. You made little pouches out of paper so every student was able to do the project. That kindness in you and your desire to help others has continued to this day. I know it will continue through college and your whole life ahead."

My mom paused and looked up at the ceiling, then she continued.

"You are going to achieve amazing things in your life and I don't have to wait until some day for you to be the person I look up to because I look up to you now. And no matter what, I will always be here for you," she ultimately said.

Tears were welling up in our eyes. We embraced each other for a long time, then I noticed that we were in the same place where I blow out my birthday candles every year and wish for more authentic moments like these. I never knew how much my mom admired me because I'm always admiring her for all of her hard work and the sacrifices she's made to give me a happy life. My heart swelled and I didn't want to let her go.

"Thank you mom, it's all because of you. I love you," I whispered.

Although I'm excited to leave for college in the fall, I still haven't processed how difficult it's going to be to part from the most important person in my life. This heartfelt conversation with my mom reminded me that it's important to know how much other people love you. Although it may be awkward, you might just find out things you've never known and deepen your relationship with the person you love the most.

Let Nature Feed Your Soul

I was the most excited for this week's Nature Challenge. I've always had a deep love for the outside, and I've even brought over 20 different species of plants into my room.

During the pandemic, we weren't allowed to go outside and that's when the number of plants in my room multiplied. What started off as 2 plants as a gift from my mom would eventually become a jungle-filled room of greenery on every table, nightstand, and bookshelf. I would adopt three new plants every month from a local store or plant nursery and squeeze them onto every available surface. Today my room is still filled with plants and I nurture every single one. There are pothos from every hook on the ceiling, succulents are mounted on my windowsill, and vines that run along my ceiling and reach the floor. I love having the beautiful green leaves brighten my room and taking deep breaths of all the fresh, clean air. Even though I ran out of space (and my mom doesn't let me buy anymore), I have so many plants to love and care for.

So for this challenge, we were asked to spend time in nature. At first, I thought I would go somewhere with a lot of plants and trees, but instead, I jumped at the opportunity to dwell in another one of nature's greatest creations: the Grand Canyon. Although it was an eight-hour drive, it was worth every second.

The afternoon sun was shining bright, so I sat down on a bench under the shade the desert trees most graciously provided. I looked across at the Grand Canyon and let the serene environment take me in.

I admired the ridges and the different hues of red and brown that intensified each time the sun shifted in the sky. I felt the air brush on my skin and blow my hair against my face. It would playfully come close to whisper in my ear then blow dust just so I wouldn't hear its secrets. As I soaked it all in, I unconsciously smiled because of how much I loved being here. This part of the world was carved from water and wind creating a striking landscape that still invoked a calmness in me, just like my room, but different.

At that moment I was fully present with my surroundings and suddenly, I remembered the little girl inside me who loved to be outside and appreciate nature. Her tiny hands were always filled with flowers, and she adored the outdoors with her great grandma.

That little girl felt like a lifetime ago. With all the trials and tribulations of school, AP classes, joining extracurriculars, working hard for grades, and rewriting college essays over and over so I could submit my best work for my college applications, I forgot how much I loved the outdoors. I felt sad that so much of my time was spent trapped within the four walls of my classrooms or my bedroom, studying and working so hard. The pressures to be this perfect student caused me to endure unmanageable stress and ignore the part of me that needs time alone with Mother Nature.

I've always known I loved the outdoors, but the Nature Challenge made me realize that it's not the beauty I admire but how it makes me feel. All those plants I brought into my room were a subconscious outlet for me to cope with my stress, and readily have what I call a *Fortress of Solitude* when we were all in quarantine. It wasn't just a new hobby; it was a way for me to build my own sanctuary.

I could have done this challenge inside my room with all my plants because I have more nature in my room than some neighborhoods do but being outdoors gave me a sense of freedom that cannot be brought into my room. Standing outside and being a small part of a big, open world, I felt like all my worries could melt away, for even just a little while. I hope you go out and find your sense of peace in nature.

In Dancing, I Found Freedom

Today is the second day of the Aerobic Exercise Challenge. I chose to run throughout this whole week, but yesterday, running was unbearable in the scorching heat. After spending the whole day sitting in class, I needed to stretch my legs. I walked into my room and pressed play on my playlist to listen to my music while I was getting ready to go for today's run. As I slid my closet door open, the song "La vie en rose" by Edith Piaf begins to play.

The first lyrics are sung.

It had been a while since I last heard this song. With the calming voice and soothing tone, it was almost as if this song was made to listen with the soul, not the ears.

I listen to the strumming of the violins and the whistling of the clarinets and flutes.

I forgot how much I used this song to help me during stressful times. It would play in the background when I was rushing to finish homework, fill out all of my college applications, and write my essays.

Although I don't know French, I can hear how passionately she sings every word.

But after all the anxiety, sleepless nights, and prolonged sittings at my desk, all I wanted to do was leave my room and run in the fresh air. I wanted to watch the sunset, run through sprinklers, and catch the falling leaves. Sadly, today was not the day for that because I couldn't ignore the blistering heat, or the hovering, heavy cloud of approaching deadlines and dozens of rewrites before my final draft.

The run had to wait but I still needed to move my body, so I opted for something else: I would dance. Alone in my room, I would dance to this song like a lone ballerina on stage giving her most graceful performance.

I start humming to the beat of the song.

I smiled. Dancing was the only time I got to stretch my stiff body and move my groggy legs, but I owned every second of it.

I can hear the soft piano playing in the background.

I turned my head towards the window and saw the blazing sun. I knew by the end of my run the hot concrete would be burning through my shoes. I looked at my phone and the song was still playing. Then a lightbulb went off in my head.

Her voice grows softer.

I slid one leg behind and lift both arms in a horizontal position. I started to go down slowly, then I lifted myself and put my legs together. I began to spin with one arm up in the air and the other down on my side.

All the instruments in unison crescendo.

My eye caught the hallway and I leapt through the door. I ran halfway down the hallway and started to slide on my socks. I was then in the kitchen, but I could still faintly hear the music.

Seeing the world in rosy pink.

I was dancing so freely that I forgot this was supposed to be a short exercise challenge.

The violins stretch their note as she strings her words.

I stopped with one knee bent forward and the other straight back. My arm was gracefully reaching for the ceiling while the other was stretching out horizontally.

Her voice stops leaving the instruments to make their final descent.

The song ended and I was panting, but still holding my final pose. I imagined an audience bursting with applause. I scurried to my room and smiled as I reached for my phone before the next song started to play.

I'm not a dancer. But during the most stressful times, I dance to get my body moving. With the Aerobic Exercise Challenge, I learned it went deeper than that. I noticed how much I love dancing for myself, for the happiness it brought me and the freedom that came with it. I'm able to freely swing my arms and leap to one side and spin on my toes and do elaborate stances without a care in the world. There's no judgmental stare, just me alone doing what makes me happy. I realized that exercising is anything that gets you moving and feeling good about yourself. So, if that means dancing with little rhythm, following a yoga routine with little flexibility, or boxing with little power, go do it and fill yourself with a feeling of accomplishment.

My Tried and True Strategy To Calmness

When the Deep Breathing Challenge was first introduced in our weekly IMPACT meeting, my mind took me back to my first therapy session. I remembered arguing with my mom that I didn't need therapy after it slipped out that I had experienced a panic attack. Then she found out it wasn't the first one and I knew she wasn't going to change her mind.

"When did your first panic attack happen?" my therapist started.

"In the fitting room of a clothing store," I responded.

I thought back to that moment. It was the summer entering my sophomore year when I was shopping for some clothes for the new school year. I received a welcoming Google Classroom message from AP Spanish Language. It was my first time taking an AP world language and I was scared.

What if I fail?
What if I can't muster my Spanish?
What if I'm not good enough to succeed?

These intrusive thoughts were racing through my head and then I couldn't breathe. My hands were trembling, my heart was racing, and tears started to blur my vision. I was alone, scared, confused, and had no coping mechanism to help me get through it.

It didn't stop there. The amount of stress I was under to be this perfect "A student" with lots of extracurriculars only worsened my panic attacks. So, the therapist that I met taught me about deep breathing.

"In... and out... just like that," my therapist told me.

I took a deep breath, held it for a few seconds, and exhaled.

"By breathing deeply, you can calm your body and feel more in control during your panic attacks and have a clearer mind," she said.

After that experience, deep breathing has become very useful to me. In heated arguments, I used to find myself taking shallow breaths to the point where I'm barely breathing. My anger fogged my brain and caused me to lash out and say regretful things to the other person. I learned that once the breaths get shorter, I must intentionally take deeper breaths to have a clearer mind to act more reasonably.

So back to the present day. When the Deep Breathing Challenge was announced I thought it was going to be a breeze. I already learned how to use it and in what ways it benefits me. But I was wrong.

This challenge was not situation-oriented. I was able to take deep breaths at any time of the day, whenever and wherever I wanted to. Breathing is an unconscious behavior our bodies do to keep us alive, but once I started to pay attention, I noticed that I go through my day without even being aware if I'm breathing at all. My breaths are naturally short and shallow, and I realized that breathing like this caused me to be on edge quicker and become easily annoyed. With deeper breaths more often, I was less agitated and more calm. As I went through the week, I made it a habit to take deep breaths regularly.

Through the challenge, I found it to be useful in any scenario. Like the time my physics teacher placed a test in front of me, and I got so nervous that I could feel my heart beating through my chest. My worries got the best of me, and I couldn't focus on the test.

Another day I got called on to answer a question. I was paying attention, but at that moment I forgot everything. I couldn't even remember the topic the teacher was presenting.

On a different day, I got into a spat with my sister, and I felt the urge to say or do something evil.

In these scenarios, I used deep breathing to help me manage the situation with a clear and composed mind. I finished the test, answered the question, and did not slap my sister. Deep breathing is a tried and true strategy to calm anyone down.

I recognized the importance of taking a moment for deep breathing. Truly, the moment we stop breathing, we stop living. But the moment we stop intentionally deep breathing, we stop giving ourselves breaks. We stop ourselves from living by our standards.

With daily deep breaths, I found myself less stressed, rarely worried, and more alive. This challenge helped me create a habit of using deep breathing any time through the day, not only in times of panic attacks and anxiety. In... and out..., that's all you need to do to take a moment for yourself.

An Interview With Author Chloe Sy-Perez

Why did you join the IMPACT Project?

My life before the IMPACT Project was around a lot of insecurity and stress. I didn't have a lot of strategies to help me cope with stressful situations, so I usually resorted to crying and napping to avoid everything. The reason I wanted to learn new strategies was that the ones I was using weren't working for me in the long term. I woke up with the same feelings and saw that nothing was resolved. Even when I would get my work done there was always some part of me that knew I could have handled that situation better. I always thought I had good mental health. But, when I realized I didn't have a lot of strategies to overcome anger and sadness and saw that I was engaging in fewer and fewer things that made me happy, I knew the IMPACT Project would provide me with the tools to overcome this. This inspired me to spend 5 months working on managing my stress better and improving my mental health to find ways to make myself happy when I'm down.

Your stories showed us some really memorable moments about building resilience and gaining confidence, but I can imagine that some challenges transformed you but weren't your favorite ones. What would you say were your favorite challenges to do?

1. Be in Nature
2. Aerobic Exercise
3. Deep Breathing

Over the course of the program, I am sure you changed in many ways. What are two of the top lessons you learned from the program that you will take with you in your life?

I learned that I am in control of my stress and have a lot of strategies to get me through hard times. I also realized that doing things for myself isn't selfish at all, it's healthy and essential and if I don't like something that's okay.

What advice would you give those who feel stressed, stuck, under pressure, or overwhelmed and don't know what to do?

Always reach out to people that you trust and never give up on yourself. There are so many tools and resources out there that want to help you. You're not alone in this, someone or something is always waiting for you.

Do you have any final words of wisdom?

Stress is how we perceive the situation; we are in control of our stress.

About the Author

Chloe Sy-Perez

Chloe Sy-Perez is a student at UCLA and the co-president of the IMPACT Project. She has a deep passion for mental health and although it's too early to know her future career, she envisions herself graduating from medical school and earning her Ph.D. to become a psychiatrist. Her passion stems from learning about brain disorders and discovering that specialized brain imaging called SPECT scans can be used to help other people change their brains and their lives. She believes that the brain is the most important organ to keep a person functioning and happy.

Chloe makes sure the people closest to her are taken care of. In other words, she is the "mom" of the group. Her favorite place is Barnes and Noble, so you know she always has a new book on hand and rewards herself by buying three more. Other than drowning in unread books, she loves to be active by running daily and going to the gym. In her free time, you can find her watering the twenty plants in her room or rewatching the Big Bang Theory. She also loves hanging out with family and friends and uncovering the best birria tacos in LA.

CHAPTER 10

Did Anyone See the Real Me?

By Samantha Sy-Perez

The IMPACT group was challenged to ask someone we knew what was one thing they admired about us. As I listened to Leanne's explanation about our weekly challenge, I silently questioned whether it would actually work. How could asking someone what they admired most about me be helpful? Even though I was unmotivated to do it, I still decided to just go for it.

The entire week, I had asked our question to my siblings and close relatives, and they had very sweet and kind answers. On the last day, I decided to ask one of my closest friends, which was terrifying. I'm typically a very reserved person, and it can be very hard for me to open up to others. As you can imagine, I was extremely nervous to ask her. I stared at my phone long and hard, then I started to type.

"Hi! I am currently involved in a group research project, and I need to ask people who know me what is one quality you admire about me. Can you help me by sharing something about me you admire?"

The text was ready to send, but I was frozen. My eyes began to water because I was staring at my phone so intensely and I had forgotten to blink. My palms turned moist as I held my phone so tightly in my hands. So many different questions raced through my mind.

What would she think about me?

Does she think I'm just looking for validation?

After 10 minutes of repetitive deleting and re-pasting the message, I finally decided to send it. I tapped the blue arrow, shut my phone off and got up from my desk. My heart raced as if my rib cage was about to burst. I tried distracting myself by resting my eyes on my bed, but that just made the waiting even worse. After what felt like an eternity, I heard my phone vibrate on my desk. *Could it be her?* I rushed over to my phone and looked down. It was my friend.

I held my breath, afraid of what she might say but I had to know. I grabbed my phone and tapped on the message. My face lit up, literally and figuratively, as my smile grew bigger and bigger.

"Samantha, I love your intelligence and your drive to always be successful no matter what you do."

Her words changed me.

Growing up, I had always been a hard worker. Whatever I did was for the sole purpose of becoming a 'better me,' and to be successful in the future. As a matter of fact, for every birthday starting at age twelve, my biggest wish has been, "I wish to be successful in the future."

As I got older, I worked even harder, but I found myself stuck in my older sister's shadow, and my hard work wasn't noticed anymore. No longer was I being told 'good job' for the things I did but scolded for the things I didn't do. In a way, I turned invisible and some days it felt like I wasn't even a part of the family. I'd hear my older sister, my younger brother, and my mom in the kitchen laughing while I sat in my room studying for a big test.

Reading my friend's words impacted me so deeply. She could have said I was nice, or kind, or a good friend. Instead, she saw the real me. She made me realize that I am my own person achieving my own successes. And, she sees how hard I work. Thanks to her,

I now know that I'm not invisible, and that the people I surround myself with actually see me in a way that is really important to me.

I'd never thought asking a friend such a simple question could be so nerve-racking, or so life-changing. But, after the challenge was over, it became clear to me that this exercise was meant to inspire us, and maybe become a more realistic mirror to view ourselves because we are often our worst critic. The point is don't let fear step in the way of trying this challenge, it might just be that the person you decide to ask will have the answer to change you.

The Day I Lost Then Found My Joy

This week we were challenged to find any good in our day to create a Joy List, which was a collection of things that brought us joy. I hoped it wouldn't be too hard.

It was a cool Thursday morning when I heard my alarm go off. Hesitant to press the snooze button, I got out of my bed and proceeded to go to the bathroom to brush my teeth and begin my day. Already proud of myself for not pushing the snooze button, my day seemed to be going pretty good so far. I wasn't even running late to school. I was even able to eat breakfast at the table rather than in the car, which is something that rarely ever happens since I'm constantly waking up late and rushing out the door.

I left my house and arrived at school with 10 minutes to spare. Since band is my zero period, arriving early is so helpful because I have a better chance of getting a good stand instead of getting stuck with a broken one.

After zero period, I met up with some of my friends and hung out with them before the first period bell rang. We had a good conversation, and we shared many laughs as one of my friends was making jokes. Once the bell rang, I took out my phone and wrote, "Laughing and socializing with my friends."

Then, things shifted. Class by class, my day just kept getting worse. First, my teachers assigned so much homework. Then, when lunch came around, I ended up getting into a heated argument with one of my closest friends.

My day was no longer going as well as it had begun, and it kept taking turns for the worse.

I got home that night just wanting the day to end. I was no longer in the happy mood the morning offered me. I felt so drained and just wanted to shut my eyes and sleep. I knew I still had to complete the challenge, so I tried to think of something else that made me cheerful but all that filled my mind were the negative things.

I opened my app and suddenly remembered that I had written something earlier in the morning. "Laughing and socializing with my friends." I had forgotten about the amazing morning I had. All my closest friends were standing in a circle shape, joking, laughing and just being dumb teenagers. Whatever I said, their ears perked up and they pointed their attention towards me so they could hear what I had to say. I was so happy at that moment.

As I sat in my bed, I thought about what happened to me throughout the day. All I was focusing on were the negative things, which made me automatically assume that I had the worst day in the world. But there were good things too.

I remembered that after I had the argument with my friend, I put on my AirPods and listened to my happy playlist because my favorite songs made me smile.

Coming home and entering my room, I saw pictures of my friends hung up, and that made me smile.

Looking at my dog peacefully sleeping with his tummy side up made me smile.

Being able to lay down on a freshly made bed after a long day of school made me smile.

Even doing my mascara made me happy.

All of these moments found their way onto my Joy List because even as small as they may be, they made me happy. Without the Joy List, I would have never even remembered the fortunate moments I had.

On the last day of the challenge, my list had become twice the size it should have been because rather than writing down one happy moment twice a day, I had written them all down. Writing them out forced my mind to focus on the positive rather than the negative.

Around a year ago, I had taken part in a journaling community. Every night at 11 pm, I would be in my room with my desk light turned on, my blue journal open, and a pen in my hand, writing my emotions away; happy, sad, whatever I needed to say, it was in my journal. Then, junior year started, and my nights were consumed with hours of studying and the occasional all-nighter so that I could keep up with the five AP classes I was taking. When I'd journal, I'd find myself focusing more on the negative things that occurred in my day, hoping they wouldn't happen again. The Joy List actually helped me focus on the positive side of my day. I would reflect on my Joy List at the end of the night and just re-read what I had written prior, and felt filled with, well, joy. And, I noticed the difference in the amount of good days I was having when I saw more positive things each day. Every day could have been a bad day in my eyes, however focusing on the good of the day allowed me to have more good days than bad.

Counting Sheep Failed Me

It was around 9 pm, a little earlier than what I was used to, but I wanted to get a good night's rest. Unfortunately, I relentlessly tossed and turned in my bed as the thought of sleep was nowhere near my mind. I just laid there, staring at the mellow gray ceiling as if it could somehow make me fall asleep quicker. I shut my eyes and began counting sheep.

One by one, bright white sheep appeared in my mind in a meadow as they jumped over a short brown fence. *One, two, three, ... seventy-*

three, seventy-four. This is hopeless, I thought. I stopped counting and just continued tossing and turning over and over, hoping to find that one position where I'd be able to just fall into a deep trance.

At the same time, different thoughts ran through my mind. *Am I missing any homework assignments? What if I'm just hungry? How did I do on my test earlier today?*

I was so confused. All throughout my school day, the only thing on my mind was coming home. I imagined myself laying on my soft bed and falling asleep, but when the time came, I could no longer sleep. I spent ten more minutes tangling myself in my blanket and throwing unnecessary stuffed animals off my bed, but still I lay awake. It seemed to me that no matter what I did, sleep wouldn't come. That's when I began to wonder whether or not I should turn on my television and watch a movie to distract myself. No, I thought to myself. I need to sleep early to wake up energized.

That's when it hit me. It was Monday and we started a new challenge today, but I had forgotten to do it. This week we were to listen to a guided meditation at bedtime. I checked the time on my alarm clock, and it was a little past ten; I still had time. I quickly grabbed my laptop from my nightstand and my AirPods from my desk. I unlocked my laptop and opened the email Angela had sent the night before with a couple of guided meditation video recommendations. I clicked on a 1 minute one just to get it over with since it was late.

OK, I'll just listen to this video and think about if it makes me feel better in any way, OK? OK.

I clicked the link, put my AirPods in and pushed play.

The sound of a soothing deep-voiced man guided me to lay still and breathe. I took several slow deep breaths, and that's when it just happened. I don't remember anything after that moment. The next thing I know, I was waking up to the sound of my alarm at 5:45am. I looked over at the side of my bed, and I saw my laptop, open but powered down, and my blue AirPods case. Why were my things in my bed and not on my desk? Then I remembered that I was listening to the guided meditation with my AirPods on before I fell asleep. I reached towards the inside of my ears and did not feel a thing. *MY AIRPODS?! Where could they have gone?* I sat up and felt around my bed, searching for them frantically when I finally felt them under my pillow. I climbed out of my bed and realized I had gotten a good night's rest. Not once do I remember waking up in the middle of the night complaining about how hot it was, or how uncomfortable my back felt.

I was hesitant about the challenge at first because I always slept in complete silence. Yet, after listening to the guided meditation, I was able to relax in my bed and actually sleep better. And being able to sleep better throughout the night let me wake up more refreshed in the morning. No longer was I waking up on the wrong side of the bed; instead, I was a more positive person in the morning. Now I know that when it's difficult for me to fall asleep at night, I'll play a quick guided meditation video. So, if you're having trouble at night being able to sleep, I recommend searching up guided meditations and trying them out. Who knows, maybe you'd end up having the best sleep of your life.

My Pillow Can Rest in Peace Now

At that moment, I had no motivation. However, I knew the challenge would only last one minute, so I decided to do it right away. Finding a song to play so that I could do the Air Boxing Challenge was the most difficult part about this task. I spent nearly ten minutes browsing through my multiple Spotify playlists before I decided on "Maneater" by Nelly Furtado. This challenge was designed to help us punch out all our frustrations and stress into the air, and even though this song would be perfect for this activity, I wasn't in a bad mood. In fact, my day had gone great, and I had even been able to hang out with some of my friends.

Just as I was about to play the song and box my heart out, my mom entered my room. The expression on my face was like I had just seen a ghost.

"What are you doing?" she asked.

"Something for Angela's project," I said, hoping she would leave quickly so I could continue the challenge.

She stood at my door for a couple of minutes, just looking at me, when she finally decided to leave. *Phew. That was a close one*, I thought to myself. The last thing I wanted was my mom entering my room as I was mid- air boxing to that song. That would have not been something she'd ever let go.

I pushed play on my phone. I placed my feet about a foot apart and just went for it. I lifted one arm and punched the air in front of me. Then, I lifted my other arm. I imagined there was a ghost in front of me and I kept hitting it. I boxed for a minute when all of a sudden, I just burst out laughing. *What am I even doing?* I clearly had never taken any boxing lessons in my life because I looked like I was swatting flies. Sweat started to form on my face, and my arms were drooping, weighing me down like a ton of bricks. *What would my mom think if she entered my room right now?* I wondered. I paused the song after 2 minutes, and just fell onto my bed.

The challenge didn't work today, I thought. But it did, just not in the way I expected.

The concept for this challenge was to try out a healthy stress-reliever, and we were to put on our favorite song and begin punching the air to release all the anger or frustration we were feeling. If I had been mad, rather than yelling and saying something I might regret later, I'd do this air boxing challenge in a heartbeat. Screaming into a pillow has been one of my go-to actions, but after a while, it doesn't relieve that much anger. This particular week, however, I wasn't mad so it felt like the challenge did not work. But, it was able to make me smile and put me in a good mood because of how silly I felt. It worked in a different way, and at the end of it, we want to keep finding ways to feel better, even unexpectedly.

An Interview With Author Samantha Sy-Perez

Why did you join the IMPACT Project?

As cliche as it sounds, I wanted to better myself and help others. Before Angela talked to me about the project she was hosting, I was in therapy. Once a week, I would meet with my therapist, and she would help me overcome some of the things I was struggling with, like my anger issues and depression. But it felt as if I needed to make more changes.

Mental health is a topic that's not talked about a lot and seems to have a negative connotation around it. However, I knew that if I took part in this project then I would be part of a movement to change that. I was excited to change the way people viewed the word "mental health" by using the experiences I had with the project and how it was able to impact me. I wanted to be an asset and be able to help others in any way possible, and that's why I decided to join the IMPACT Project.

Your stories showed us some really memorable moments about building resilience and gaining confidence, but I can imagine that some challenges transformed you but weren't your favorite ones. What would you say were your favorite challenges to do?

1. Create Joy List
2. Be in Nature
3. Guided Meditation

What do you now know about your ability to overcome hard things?

I know that for me, it takes time to overcome hard things. I would expect myself to get over the hard things pretty quick and when I didn't I would get mad at myself. I have now realized that in order to overcome hard things I need to give myself time to feel the emotions that come with it and get angry or sad, then I can really let it go; I don't keep anything bottled up now.

What advice would you give those who feel stressed, stuck, under pressure, or overwhelmed and don't know what to do?

For those who feel stressed, stuck, under pressure, or overwhelmed it may feel like you're sinking and there's no way to get back to the surface. Believe me, I've been there. But there's always a way out. You have the power to change that. No one is going to pull you out, you're going to have to do it. Sure, there may be people around you who will be there to help, but at the end of the day, it's on you to decide if you want to better yourself. When you're feeling stressed, take some time to just take a deep breath. Stop what you're doing, untense your jaw and shoulders and just relax. Breathe in and out while trying to clear your head. After this moment, make yourself a plan. Get out a piece of paper and make a checklist. Write down everything that needs to be completed, and order them from the most time it will take to the least. Don't be afraid to take a break and go outside; be in nature. It'll help to calm your mind, start fresh ideas flowing, and re-energize as you move through your list of things to do.

Do you have any final words of wisdom?

Take care of yourself first before taking care of others, because you matter. Self-care can be whatever soothes your soul.

About the Author

Samantha Sy-Perez

Samantha Sy-Perez is a rising senior in high school living in southern California. In college, she hopes to combine her passions in computer science, education, business, and psychology. Her dream is to run her own business teaching technology skills and leadership to young people.

During her summer, she coaches rising 8th graders how to code at a virtual all-girl camp. In school, she's part of the Coding Club, and the Environmental Activism Club where she advocates for others to be environmentally aware. She is also a flutist in her school's marching band and participated in multiple competitions where her school won first place.

The IMPACT Project helped her manage time better, so now she spends most of her days stress-free. As the Marketing and Media Director, she created the website and started a podcast called "Many Ways to Be Okay" to spread awareness about mental health to more people.

Samantha loves spending time on self-care, teaching her Shih Tzu new tricks, reading mystery thriller books, and feeding her unhealthy Starbucks addiction. She would say that the best part of any day would be being able to hang out with her closest friends and family.

CHAPTER 11

'Bro, What Does Success Mean To You?'

By Jay Choi

Imagine you walked up to your friend and asked them, "Hey. What's up? How are you doing?"

How would they respond to you?

If I were to guess, I bet that they said, "Meh, ummm, nothing much," or, "Good, how about you?"

These kinds of short, boring, meaningless greetings and conversations never lead to anything deeper, and honestly, they make you yawn. But this week's challenge was called "Conversation Starters." The challenge's purpose was to have a deeper conversation and get to know more about others using open-ended questions.

When I first heard about this challenge, I underestimated it, and I thought this would be a piece of cake. I mean, I always talk to my friends anyway, how hard can this be? I was even given a list of questions that I could use, and it all seemed simple enough. My intention was to only talk to my friends and family because it is easier and more convenient.

But when I went up to talk to my friends, my question came out of the blue.

"Bro... What does success mean to you?"

My friends were a little bit confused because I'm the jokester in my friend group, and they were thinking they didn't understand my joke; they looked at me with confusion. Like, why would a jokester suddenly talk about life? To be honest, my friends were worried if I was going through something in my life. I reassured them I was fine.

As I kept talking to my friends and family, I understood the challenge even better, and started to feel more comfortable. I felt like it was time for me to get out of my comfort zone, and I thought that it wasn't a challenge if I didn't feel challenged.

Then I saw this girl.

I knew her name because she was in my class, but I didn't know her as a person. She was drawing a beautiful piece for her art class. I decided I would use a Conversation Starter question with her. I just hoped to have a nice conversation for a few seconds, but then fear got to me. I wondered, *'is this a good or bad idea?'* My mind was flooded with negative thoughts about how it can go wrong.

What if I look bad?
What if I stutter and say some weird things?
What if I look like a creep or other people think I have a crush on her?

A bunch of stupid and useless thoughts came through my mind. Even though I knew things could turn out badly, I still decided to go talk to her because, why not?

I was nervous and heard my heart pounding inside my body.

I took a deep breath.
Then another one.
Then one more.

Finally, I went over to her. I knew what I wanted to say, and I knew my intention was to ask her about her art, but when I stood beside her, my brain froze and I didn't know what to say anymore.

I tried to speak, but my nervousness got me stuck in a hole filled with darkness.

Then my brain started yelling at me. *'Why? Why did you do this?'*

It was too late. I was already next to her and if I turned away, I would look weird.

Then, she looked at me and her facial expression was like, "what the heck?"

She was also giving me some, "What do you want?" look, you know?

I knew I needed to spit out some words at least or else she would think I was a weirdo. My heart kept pounding, sweat started coming out of my pores, and I started to feel dizzy.

Finally, I squeezed out some words. "Hey, wassup?"

"Nothing much..." she replied with an equal amount of awkwardness.

My brain finally relaxed a bit, and I finally found some words. "I really like your drawing, What are you making?" After I said it, I was relieved like a clogged toilet that was able to get unclogged.

She responded back with thank you. Then she asked me if I knew how to draw, and it caught me off-guard, but I answered back with, "Nah... I suck at it."

As our conversation went on, I totally forgot about that moment of nervousness a few seconds ago. Surprisingly, our chat lasted longer than I expected. It was fun talking to her and I realized what an awesome person she was. It wasn't like *I had a crush on her* but I enjoyed getting to know my classmate.

I sat down to get ready for class and all my negative thoughts and feelings were gone; my body was completely back to normal.

In the end, it was a great idea for me to go up to her and talk. After the good conversation, I realized that it wasn't so bad! And I was able to get out of my comfort zone, meet a really nice person, and give her a compliment that hopefully made her feel good about her drawing.

I really enjoy getting to know other people, even though I'm always awkward at first. I spend a lot of time looking for the right moment to jump in and make a connection with them. The majority of people usually greet each other using simple 'yes or no' questions that take no effort and often lack meaning but using Conversation Starters really helped me have deeper conversations with my family, friends, and even acquaintances.

So, next time you're talking to your friends about Breaking Bad (a great Netflix show), I encourage you to go up to them and ask, "Bro, what does success mean to you?"

The One Thing Gaming Could Never Give Me

This week's challenge was called "Be in Nature." This challenge's purpose was to just be in nature, present in our thoughts and feelings, rather than being on our addictive and distractive phones scrolling through social media or playing video games in our rooms.

The challenge of being in nature would be easy. The challenge of being off my phone would be hard. If I could get over the first five minutes of temptation and fight off the boredom from not having my phone, I would be fine, I thought. I sat down on a park bench and had to actively resist checking my phone because it was such a big part of my life and my habits.

I have been playing video games since I was five years old. My brother would play and I would watch him, asking so many questions to understand how it all worked. I became more interested in games as I got older, and I played on my computer and on my phone. Then I found social media, and I loved scrolling through my feeds online, seeing what my friends were doing and watching funny videos to share with them.

When I sat on the bench at the park, the first five-minutes ran like Patrick's stone pet from SpongeBob. I knew that time was passing, but at the same time, it felt like it wasn't. It felt like I was stuck in a different dimension where I could move, but time was frozen.

When the five minutes passed, I wasn't as tempted anymore, so I stood up, looked around with a blank stare, and asked myself, "So... *what should I do for the next twenty-five minutes?*" I sat back down.

Time was moving so SLOW. The first five minutes crawled, so I knew the next twenty-five minutes would feel like forever. Then, I had thousands of thoughts running through my brain.

'What would I normally be doing at 5:37 P.M?'

'How would I be doing on the latest game that I'm obsessed with?'

'I've had a long week; maybe I'd be taking a short nap in my bed.'

'I wonder what people are posting online that I am missing right now.'

When I thought about my thoughts, I realized how much time I spend on things like games and social media. Day after day, I spent my free time doing these same things because I really enjoyed them. But my dad was always scolding me for using my time like this because he wanted me to see my time as something to value, not something to waste. Being on my phone never seemed like a waste to me.

I had only been sitting in nature for ten minutes, but I hadn't really enjoyed it because I was thinking about all the things I would do online when the thirty minute timer went off and I could leave the park.

Suddenly it hit me and I understood the meaning behind my dad's words. *Time is so valuable, and more importantly, we can never get it back.*

Sitting on the bench, I felt a little bit ashamed of myself for spending almost all my free time playing games and scrolling, but there was no point in feeling bad about it anymore, it was in the past. So, I asked myself, *'what do I want to do now?'*

Let's think about it.

One day has twenty-four hours and during those twenty-four hours, we hopefully use about eight hours to sleep. Perhaps we spend two or three hours for breakfast, lunch, and dinner, which includes making the meal, eating it, and cleaning up after it. That is a total of ten or eleven hours. And for me, as a teenager, I have to go to school for seven hours. With school added in, we have used eighteen hours. There are six hours left, and if we are really lucky, they are ours and we can use them however we want. We can work out, study, rest, be with family, help around the house, play music, and much more. Personally, I have mostly used my time for gaming and in other unproductive ways. As I kept reflecting on my choices, I realized that I needed to get my butt straight and start to use my time more wisely.

I had never done a Nature Challenge like this before where I went to the park to sit on a bench for thirty minutes. I wasn't sure what I would do there, and I was surprised that I spent time thinking about my life. In a way, this challenge changed me a lot. I was able to learn more about what was important in my life, re-evaluate how I spend my time, and decide that I wanted to learn more about myself to grow even more. Overall, it's okay for us to spend some time online, either on social media or gaming, because it does bring us joy. We love our phones, and they love us back! But there has to be a balance with activities that don't involve your phone. And, if you try going into nature, you just might forget about your phone because spending time in nature is almost always a good use of your time.

Pushing Myself Through the 'Dread'

This week's challenge was to do an "Aerobic Exercise" and get your heart pumped up. Basically, it is a cardio workout that I could do while listening to music so that we could test if we would feel accomplished and fresh in our minds.

My thought on this challenge was that it would be very simple because it only had to last one or two minutes per day. We don't realize how fast one or two minutes pass, so how hard could it be? I wondered whether I should go jogging or do jumping jacks. I just wanted to have something simple that would get my heart pumping.

I chose jumping jacks. For the first ten seconds, I was fine. By the time I reached the one-minute mark, I had hit a wall of pain and exhaustion.

"Ughhh... Arghh..." My heart was pumping, and I was breathing so heavy, but I kept going. I was surprised that jumping jacks made me feel so exhausted, but not necessarily better. I don't know why these challenges sound so easy but become really difficult once I actually do them.

The next day, I decided to go running. I thought it would be a lot easier and wouldn't tire me as easily as jumping jacks did. I remembered how my dad used to teach me how to run like a true runner, giving me so many tips and techniques. When he tried to explain things to me, I remember saying in my mind, "Oh my god... Here we go again..." I don't think I really listened, and it was so long ago, I couldn't recall any of his suggestions. Sadly, I didn't have his advice to help me on my run that day.

After a few stretches and deep breaths, I grabbed my phone and got my mindset ready. I turned on my timer and I was ready to become a menace. This time I decided to run as fast as I could for one minute, then jog for the rest. I drank a sip of water and started my timer

I started with a burst, running with my full energy. I stayed focused on my breathing and my steps. I inhaled and exhaled. Repeat. I ran for about 30 seconds, then I started to feel pain in my stomach. I had forgotten it happens to me all the time and I never figured out why. It's like a dull knife poking me in my left belly. I was mad at my body, like, *are you serious??? This is going to ruin my running.* I really, really hated this feeling and I wished that it stopped but I couldn't control it.

At that moment, I decided that I couldn't let this pain beat me because I had my own respect for myself. I kept running until the timer hit one minute, then I started jogging. Thankfully, the pain started to fade away. I was able to gain focus on my running once again and I kept on going. Forty-eight more seconds. I couldn't wait to finish this challenge because I just wanted to stop exercising and be lazy again. I looked up at the sky, and down at the ground. Then, I looked up again and I noticed the sky was a beautiful orange and a charming shade of blue; my run was during a really nice sunset and I almost missed seeing the sky.

When my timer finally rang, I stopped. I was breathing so heavily, and my legs were about to fall apart, yet I felt so energized. And the feeling of running was marvelous. Well, actually I felt mummified because my mouth was completely dry and gritty. I guzzled some water and I tasted victory. After a moment of recovery, my mind was fresh and for some strange reason, I was ready to run again. Even though it was tiring, I really love the feeling when I do something that fires up my spirit inside me.

I rested for a few minutes, and I ran again for two minutes. I felt refreshed and energized and free. I first thought that this challenge would be boring.

But I was wrong. I had fun challenging myself and I was able to gain confidence and motivation from completing this challenge, which I dreaded at first.

The Mind Will Quit Before the Body

The challenge for this week was called, 'Hold a Plank.' This challenge's purpose was to hold a plank as long as we can and observe how it can strengthen us mentally because we learned that sometimes our mind will quit before our body does. This challenge was to help us get stronger mentally because whenever there is something that we can't really endure, we just give up. Doing this challenge was a way we could improve and strengthen our mental health in a positive and healthy way.

My first feeling about this challenge was, '*Uh-oh... I'm going to have a hard time...*' I tried planking before, and I remembered it was not the best experience. I didn't want to feel that serious pain in my abs again but this was our challenge, so I told myself, '*This is going to be inevitable, so I need to do it.*'

My first goal was to hold a plank for at least forty-five seconds and increase it little by little each day. I had done thirty seconds before, so I wanted to do more. My mind had so many thoughts.

Should I add it to my regular workout routine?
No, I don't want to add it to my routine.

I want to have abs.
But I don't want the pain.

I don't like planks.
But I love challenges.

Remembering that I need to do this challenge for a whole week gave me goosebumps. I tried to think about this in a positive way so I could enjoy it, but it was hard because I knew they caused me agony. I mean, this was a *challenge*, so of course, it would be really hard.

It was time for me to start this thing. On my first day, I knew I had to take it easy. I first sat down and asked myself, '*Am I really ready?*' My mind was ready, but my body wasn't. Finally, I just decided to do it.

The first few seconds were really fine. But as time went on, it was like an inferno in my body. The ache started to get stronger, and I felt the burn. I groaned quietly. I didn't want to sound weak because I knew I was better than this.

At the twenty-five second mark, I really wanted to give up. But I also wanted to hold it longer. My face looked red and squished, like an old tomato.

Then I remembered words from our Sunday meeting: *sometimes our mind will quit before our body does.*

I changed my thoughts with strong and encouraging words.

'Just a little bit more!'
'A few more seconds!'
'Just enjoy the burn, man, it's okay'

But my motivation only lasted about ten seconds. As a believer, I have faith and love God, so I spoke to Him, saying *'Please God, just fast forward this time... Why do you only slow down time when I am suffering?'* I held onto my plank pose a little bit more.

As soon as my timer rang at forty-five seconds, I collapsed on the floor and waited for the pain in my abs to go away. Then I told myself I couldn't be funny for the rest of the day because I remembered that when my ab muscles are burning, laughing will hurt.

In my opinion, this Plank Challenge wasn't that bad, but it was different than I thought. I thought that I would feel the burn and just be so focused on the pain while holding the plank; that was true on the first day. But then with each day of practice, I learned how to maintain my focus and have more positive thoughts. One big thing I noticed was that I stopped overthinking and imagining the worst, and I started to have an *'I'm in control of this'* mindset. Like, small disturbing things that used to affect me no longer bothered me at all. I started to say, *'It's whatever... Pfft. It should be fine as long as I don't die.'*

From this challenge, I also learned that I'm resilient, motivated, and determined, and I can do hard things. Many people give up easily if something affects them negatively. Doing this challenge taught me that I can endure hard or uncomfortable things and build confidence by having a stronger mentality.

You should try holding a plank, too! I promise you that it will enhance your mental health, but you will experience HELL on your way there. Do you want to become stronger or nah? Your choice.

An Interview With Author Jay Choi

Why did you join the IMPACT Project?

Before I started the IMPACT Project, I had a lot of stress. It kept on building up in my mind and I had nowhere to put it. I was a teenager who wanted to know how to manage stress, overwhelm, and many pressures. I wished that there could be a great solution where I could relieve my stress in a healthier way. I remember I was suffering from the pain of school and it gave me a lot of comfort after using the breathing technique. I started to gain confidence and optimism that this project could help me in many ways in my life. This motivated and inspired me to stay for five months with commitment and have an impact on my personal development and leadership skills.

Your stories showed us some really memorable moments about building resilience and gaining confidence, but I can imagine that some challenges transformed you but weren't your favorite ones. What would you say were your favorite challenges to do?

1. Conversation Starters
2. Aerobic Exercise
3. Hold a Plank

Over the course of the program, I am sure you changed in many ways. How would you describe yourself before and after the IMPACT Project? What are the biggest changes you notice about yourself?

After all of these weeks, I noticed that I am a more positive, motivated, and healthier person than before. Every week when we completed our challenges, I started feeling like I was a new "Jay" because I was growing in confidence. Doing all these new activities that I haven't done before made me feel a total new person. Finishing these challenges with commitment made me feel like a "champion".

Before the project, I would also always be worried and lose a lot of confidence thinking about other people's judgment and criticism. Now, I don't really worry about what others think; I care more about myself and how I can accomplish my goals.

What advice would you give those who feel stressed, stuck, under pressure, or overwhelmed and don't know what to do?

For those people who feel stressed, I suggest you go for a walk and breathe in some fresh air to make you calm. If you have a dog, then go for a walk with your dog and play with them. If you ever feel like you are stuck, overwhelmed, or pressured, take one step at a time or break down the steps so you can easily know where you can start. Knowing where you can start can help you feel less stuck because you can see your progress and this can help you achieve your goal faster and better.

Do you have any final words of wisdom?

"You never know how strong you are, until being strong is your only choice" - Bob Marley.

This quote makes me feel like I can still keep going. Even though I am going through a lot in my life, I can still go on because I know deep inside that I am very strong. I never know until I recognize myself putting 100 percent or even 200, 300, 400, or 500 percent of my will and effort.

One thing I learned from this IMPACT Project is that everyone can fall once, twice or multiple times in their life, however not all know how to get up and continue. For that, we need to get up and keep on trying our best to succeed and reach that goal.

About the Author

Jay Choi

Jay Choi is a rising senior attending high school in southern California. He is a positive guy who loves to perform acts of kindness and help those around him. He enjoys boxing, listening to music, hanging out and having fun with his friends while making new friends along the way.

At school, he participates in many events to support other communities such as vaccine clinics, Asian American Association, and Key Club.

Within the IMPACT Project, as a key contributor to bringing mental health awareness and as the co-host of the accompanying podcast "Many Ways to Be Okay," Jay was selected to be the Director of Special Projects. The IMPACT Project helped Jay discover that no one is alone in their hard times, and now more than ever, we are all ONE team and we need to fight mental health issues together.

Jay believes that mental wellness is an important issue in today's world and he wants his career to be helping others in this area. He believes that his gifts of being kind, compassionate, and friendly can help him encourage others to find their happiness.

CHAPTER 12

Getting Revenge on an Invisible Force
By Cedrick Kim

Have you ever had low expectations when trying something new? Like food for example. Someone offers you some new interesting-looking dish, and at first, you hesitate because you don't know what you're getting yourself into. However, after trying that new dish, it becomes one of the best things you've eaten all day. That was pretty much my experience with this challenge. It was Sunday night and I was on Zoom listening to our weekly meeting. Heading into week six of the IMPACT Project, I had pretty much gotten the hang of the weekly routine: we get a new challenge every Sunday, do the challenge throughout the week, record the results, and see how the challenge may have affected us. Most of the challenges so far had been pretty good, and I was interested to see what was in store for us this week.

When the challenge was revealed, everyone was pretty surprised. 'Air boxing? Is that what I think it is?' I thought. Just then, the theme song to Rocky comes on and Angela and Leanne start to explain what this week's challenge is all about. For one minute each day, for six days, we will box into the air, then record how it affected us. I remember ending the meeting and sitting in my chair thinking, *this is gonna be an interesting week.*

On Monday, I got home from practice, did some homework, and remembered that I had to air box. I went into my room, closed the door, and standing there alone, I proceeded to punch and duel the air. Throwing jabs and uppercuts I punch my invisible opponent and finally, the timer goes off, and the awkward silent match is over. I stood there feeling a little silly and besides my heart pumping a little bit faster, I didn't feel any difference. I just went back to my desk and started to work on my homework again.

On Tuesday, the day was pretty much the same as Monday. I came home, worked on my homework, and remembered to do the challenge. I stood up, went to my room, and had another one-minute boxing match with the air. The results were still the same; I finished air boxing and went back to what I was doing before without feeling much of a difference.

On Wednesday, I was woken up to my phone screaming; actually, it was my alarm, but it felt like it was screaming at me. I had stayed up really late the night before working on two different assignments and trying to study for my first-period test. I sluggishly forced myself out of bed and got ready for school. I took the test, but I was disappointed because I knew I could have prepared myself better. The rest of the day goes by like a blur: more classes, more assignments, more tests, and more frustration boiling up within me. However, the day wasn't over yet. I had volleyball practice, which is something that usually lifts my spirits, but that day I was making every mistake possible: missing hits on perfect sets, missing digs right to me, and missing serves. It felt like the theme of the day was, 'How much can Cedrick be annoyed in one day?'

I left volleyball practice with my frustration bubbling over. I got home, threw my bag on the floor, and sat on my bed with my hands over my face. I just wanted the day to end.

Then I remembered this week's challenge and thought it would be a good idea to start it right away. I stood up and once again I started to throw punches, but this time it was different. My eyes are closed and I'm not just punching the air, my whole day was my opponent. This time with my boxing, I'm getting my revenge. I throw jabs, uppercuts, and other improvised combos, unloading a fury of punches against all the things that went wrong in my day.

When my timer went off, I sat on my bed and collected my thoughts. I chuckled a sheepish laugh and thought to myself, '*I can't believe that actually worked.*' Standing by myself and punching the air really worked. I felt better. My head felt clear. My face wasn't scrunched up with anger. I actually felt a difference.

This silly challenge of punching air for a whole minute actually made me feel better. I wasn't trapped in these feelings of anger and frustration like in the past. I now had an outlet to release these pent-up feelings. Instead of imploding with these frustrating emotions, I could explode and release them in a healthier way. This experience really helped me open my eyes to these challenges. I no longer saw these challenges as just activities to do and record, I now saw them as potential outlets or ladders that could help me climb out of whatever hole I felt trapped in. This experience really got me thinking to myself, "If a silly challenge like this had an impact on me, what other challenges could do the same?"

I Am Home

This week, our challenge in the IMPACT Project was to create a joy list. A joy list is exactly what it sounds like, listing all the things that bring you joy. I was excited about this week's challenge because I had never tried making a joy list before so I was eager to see how it would turn out. I spent the week creating my joy list and writing the things that bring me joy. I added things such as my family, my home, my friends, my dog, movies, video games, food, etc...

However, it took me until the end of the week to realize that this challenge wasn't really that effective for me. Yes, when writing new things down on the list, a smile forms on my face and I'm happy, but in moments of frustration, stress, or sadness, it doesn't really help. Throughout the week whenever I felt stressed or frustrated, I tried thinking of things on my list to bring a little joy into my mind. I would think of my friends, family, movies, and video games and just think, 'Yeah, that's great,' but it didn't really change how I felt.

One day when I got home, I went through my list again, looking at each entry trying to see which one brought me true joy. After reading it over and over, I finally saw it. A four-letter word sitting there on the page: home.

When I was making my joy list, I remembered putting *home* on my list, but not really thinking much about it. On this day, I sat on the floor really thinking about my home, and I didn't realize how much joy my home brought me.

My home was my escape, a place where I could just be me. Walking into my nice, clean room, free of school work and papers, I could relax. My walls were covered with my posters depicting characters from my favorite shows and movies. My room was filled with things that bring me joy, and it is my sanctuary to retreat to after a long and stressful day. Looking back through the years, the thing that would get me through the long hours and grueling work was opening the door to my room and just collapsing on my bed. I had just never noticed that before.

In this challenge, I had been trying to think of all these new and exciting things that bring me joy, but I overlooked the most important and somewhat simple one. This challenge helped me realize that sometimes the most important things in life aren't the biggest or most eye-appealing things, it's the simple stuff. Whenever I feel stressed or tired, I just have to think about the warm and joyful feeling of being home.

True Growth Takes Time and Dedication

It was Sunday night again, which meant it was time for our weekly meeting. I remember scrambling to clear my desk, get my computer, and log onto Zoom. At this point, it was already week ten of the IMPACT Project. Reaching week ten, I was pretty used to the weekly routine by now, but even though the IMPACT Project's weekly routine was nice and smooth, it didn't mean my school routine was. I had assignments to turn in, tests to study for, and a whole lot of things going on outside of this project, so I was both excited and relieved when I heard about this week's challenge.

For this week, we got to choose an aerobic exercise to do throughout the week and record how it made us feel. I confidently sat back in my chair, happy that this week's challenge would be "easy". I'm a pretty active guy, so getting some exercise seemed fun and easy for me.

I chose to do push-ups for the entire week for my exercise, but push-ups aren't technically an aerobic exercise. After asking Angela and Leanne about it, they said it was okay to do. I chose to do push-ups because I like them and they're relatively easy for me to do. I thought to myself, 'Sure I haven't done them for a while but it shouldn't be a big deal.'

The next day, I dropped myself on the floor, got my hands into position, and started doing those push-ups. My goal was to do at least twenty-five push-ups, so I started counting. One, two, three, four.

Right when I got to twenty I thought, 'Wow, this is actually kind of hard.' I recalled a time when doing forty push-ups was easy for me, but because I stopped doing them, they had become hard.

Using all the strength left in my trembling arms, I slowly banged out five more and then laid down on the floor. However, lying there on the floor of my room with my chest and arms burning, I felt good. Even with a small task like this, it felt good to accomplish a goal that I had set for myself. It felt good to be getting in my push-ups again, and I felt eager to do them again tomorrow.

This simple exercise had such an impact on me because of the metaphor I found in it. When trying to grow or change in life, I often expect fast results. I go to bed thinking that tomorrow I will be a *new me* and when I rise from my bed the next morning *a new and improved Cedrick* will be there, but that's just not true. Growing is something that takes time and hard work. Just like those push-ups, when you want to start making changes in your life and grow, it's going to be hard at first. However, the more consistently you do them, the easier they get, and the more you can do. If you really want to grow as a person, or grow at a skill, or grow at whatever, you have to be committed. It takes hard work, it takes determination, and it takes dedication to see those results. But, it's that hard work and dedication that makes it all worth it. In the end when you see how far you've come, when you finally make it to the top of that mountain, you will stand there, satisfied, because you know all the things you did to get there.

An Umbrella That Protects Me From the Storm

Finally starting the IMPACT Project I had no idea what to expect. It was week one of the IMPACT Project and it was our first meeting on our "sacred Sunday night". I checked my hair, made sure my computer was charged, and then logged into Zoom.

To be honest, I was a bit nervous. I had never done anything like this before.

I didn't know anyone else who was participating in this project.

I didn't know how this would go or what these other kids would be like.

Nonetheless, I pushed all those thoughts away as the discussion got started. At the end of the meeting, we had gotten our first weekly challenge to try and it seemed really easy. We were assigned to do this deep breathing exercise. We were to take long deep breaths, but it was more than that. We were told to think of an imaginary box, and imagine a little ball taking four seconds to roll along each side of the box. As the ball rolled down the first side, we were to inhale for the four seconds. When the ball rolled down the second side, we were to hold our breath until the imaginary ball reached the next corner, or the duration of four seconds. When the ball rolled down the third side, we were to exhale slowly, and when the ball rolled along the fourth side, we were to hold our breath without air in our lungs. Then we would repeat the box breathing all over again, taking these long intentional breaths in and out for only a minute.

Hearing this, I was excited. I had heard about these breathing exercises before, and I was curious to see if they would actually work in helping us feel better in any way. In the early parts of that week, I was a little skeptical. I was breathing and doing the exercise but felt no real difference.

It wasn't until later in the week that I really felt this challenge make a difference. Normally, feelings of stress, frustration, and tiredness would hang around my head, raining down a storm of feelings and emotions, but not this time. No, this time I had an "umbrella" to protect me from this storm. Whenever I felt stressed out or even tired, I tried doing this breathing exercise, and while I was doing the exercise, I really focused on doing each of the breaths moving around the imaginary box. I was really focusing on how each one felt, and what it was doing to my mind and body. I was surprised, but it actually helped.

I still use this challenge even today. Now I don't use it every day all the time, but when I find myself in moments of stress or frustration like preparing to take a big test or having to wait in the ridiculously long line at lunch, I use this technique to help relieve those feelings. Something as simple as breathing, which we do every day, has the potential to help us feel so much better. When we take time to stop and focus on our breathing and really think about the intentionality behind it, it can really open our eyes to what something as simple as breathing can really do.

An Interview With Author Cedrick Kim

Why did you join the IMPACT Project?

Life before the IMPACT Project was pretty mediocre. Junior year was turning out to be exactly what everyone said it would be: a year filled with stress and overwhelming thoughts about college and the future. A combination of the long hours, the uninteresting classes, and the pressure and stress of maintaining grades made me develop these hateful feelings towards school, and made me see school as a necessary evil. I felt stuck in this cage of anger and frustration. Wishing every day that I could take interesting classes, or that school was better somehow.

Then I was introduced to the IMPACT Project. I thought learning about mental health and trying different strategies to improve my mental health sounded like a good idea. Over the course of the project however, I didn't just learn a couple of challenges, I grew a little more as a leader and in my leadership skills. The IMPACT Project has helped me realize that I don't have to be or feel stuck; there are strategies, people, and tips out there that can help me build a ladder out of this metaphorical hole that I'm stuck in, and building that ladder takes time, it's a process. Nobody is going to build that ladder overnight, it takes one step at a time, and these tips and challenges in this project could be those small steps for you. In order to build that ladder, and bring it into existence, all it takes is building that first step.

Your stories showed us some really memorable moments about building resilience and gaining confidence, but I can imagine that some challenges transformed you but weren't your favorite ones. What would you say were your favorite challenges to do?

1. Be in Nature
2. Unplug Before Sleeping
3. Deep Breathing

Over the course of the program, I am sure you changed in many ways. What are some top lessons you learned from the program and your biggest takeaway that you will take with you in your life?

The two top things that I learned is to have an open mind, and that hard work and determination pay off. These two things for me kind of go hand in hand, but having an open mind applies to all the challenges that I did. Having an open mind and being willing to try these challenges really helped me discover some things that can really benefit me in my life. Then two, having determination and doing the hard work paid off. By sticking with the project and doing the challenges, I reaped all these benefits and had an amazing time learning, growing, and connecting with people that are great.

My biggest takeaway is that there are some amazing people out in this world, and that I have the ability now to be one of those people for someone else. I can take what I learned, and all the strategies and skills I learned, and teach those things to others. I can be an Angela or Leanne for someone else, and really impact their lives. Then they can go on and have an impact on others, and the cycle goes on.

What advice would you give those who feel stressed, stuck, under pressure, or overwhelmed and don't know what to do?

Feeling stuck.

It's something that everyone has experienced in their life, and it sucks because you feel like you're trapped in this cage and you have no way of getting out. Well, I'm here to tell you that you're not stuck forever, and there are ways to get out.

My first point of advice is to remember that you are not alone. No matter what you're feeling, no matter what you're going through, there are people out there who are going through similar things that you are. Feeling like you are the only one who is feeling stuck is a dangerous way to think. Every person you see in your day is either trapped in their own version of a cage or they have been before, so they know what it feels like.

This brings me to my second point, to try and talk to someone. Whether it's your parents, a friend, or a teacher, studies show that simply talking about our problems and sharing our thoughts with someone we trust can be profoundly healing. It can reduce stress, and provide a way for you to process your thoughts and feelings. You might even be introduced to new perspectives and ideas that might help you solve your problems.

Talking about your feelings and problems isn't a sign of weakness, it's actually a sign of strength because it takes courage to take those first steps and get the help you need.

Do you have any final words of wisdom?

One quote that has really helped me is to "keep an open mind." I had to practice this throughout the whole IMPACT Project.

Being introduced to and having to do these challenges I had never heard of, I remember being a bit hesitant to some of them at first. I thought, *will this really help?*

If I had stopped myself from trying these new things because they were new or sounded silly, I never would have found easy and simple tips to help me feel better. By keeping an open mind and trying these challenges I found some that really helped make me feel better when I'm stressed or frustrated. Practicing this has really helped me to be more willing to try new things.

My words of wisdom to you are to keep an open mind and be willing to try new things, because even though they might sound simple, or silly, they might just surprise you.

About the Author

Cedrick Kim

Cedrick Kim is a rising senior trying his best to finish strong. He is involved with many leadership activities at school, like giving visitor tours and being an ambassador in the international student program.

After having a rough start to his junior year, Cedrick joined the IMPACT Project looking for ways to grow in personal development and as a leader. He started as a member and quickly ascended to become the Director of Outreach. Through the project, he learned many new strategies, especially ways to reduce his stress and improve his mental health. Along the course of the project, he also grew in his leadership skills and formed new connections with other like-minded people in the group, and his social circle grew.

When he's not doing challenges like air boxing or deep breathing, he plays volleyball with his friends and travels LA trying to find new and delicious foods to eat. Cedrick dreams of finding a job that he loves doing, and that allows him to connect with people on a more personal level. He also hopes to give back to his family and friends who helped him get this far in life.

CHAPTER 13

The Soldiers Were Preparing for Battle

By Aiden Jung Won Chang

For about a week and a half, I had been studying for my biology midterm. I'm usually an anxious person at test time, but the pressure this time felt like the weight of a mountain. Biology was my hardest subject, and even though I had studied every section several times, I had the lingering feeling I hadn't studied enough. Plus, this wasn't just any test, it was the mid-term, worth 10 percent of our entire grade. I also had extra pressure since my grade was on the borderline between A- and B+, and I really wanted to end with an A-, at the least.

As luck would have it, biology was my last class of the day, which means my nervousness exponentially increased *every* hour. By lunchtime, I felt as if I was going to pass out. When the last period bell rang out, it was as if a commander had yelled *'Soldiers, get ready for battle,'* right before the war was about to begin.

I sat down in my biology class, unable to remember anything I had studied. I felt like I was a soldier, and this was my march to the front lines. I tried to calm my nerves down, mostly by talking to my friends, but that didn't help much. As our teacher handed out the tests, I felt as if the world was turning upside down. Instead of thinking about the test in front of me, I was focusing on all the other assignments waiting to be finished tonight at home. I was getting hot and sweaty, feeling so overwhelmed that I just wanted to go home and hide under my sheets.

Then, I remembered another thing I had to do tonight. Aw shoot, I have the IMPACT Project challenge to finish when I get home.

At first, I was really annoyed since that just added to my already full plate of things I had to do. Then, I remembered that this week's challenge was 'deep breathing,' and I thought to myself, *'maybe, just maybe, could that help me now?'* For your reference, this is a bit different from the deep breathing most people are familiar with. This is when you breathe deeply in for five seconds, hold your breath for five seconds, then let it out.

I looked down at the test and I really couldn't even read the questions, my eyes were blurry. I rubbed them and then looked again, and I wasn't sure I knew any of the answers. I had to try something. I took a few short moments (which felt like ten years) to slowly breathe in and out, in and out, in and out.

For the first couple of breaths, there wasn't really any improvement, so I considered quitting. I thought, *'I have a limited time for this test, I need to start it instead of wasting precious minutes doing something pointless.'* But I just wasn't ready to start writing on my paper, so I kept on breathing.

Slowly, surprisingly, I felt increasingly better! Each time I took a breath out, it seemed as if my shoulders were loosening. I could feel my muscles relaxing, and my brain clearing like smoke after you spray some water on it. My heart started pumping slower, and I stopped feeling like my eyes would pop out from my stress headache.

Was this test as hard as I was making it? Was I really unprepared? Before I started deep breathing, I felt like I was facing an enemy soldier without any bullets in my weapon, and I couldn't do anything about it. But, after a few minutes of slow, intentional breathing, it was like I was given the bullets to defend myself; I had everything I needed.

If my studying and all the stored information in my brain were my weapons, then my newfound confidence, which came from my breathing, could help me "defeat" the test. I looked down at my paper and the problems on the test started to make sense. I felt a lot more confident about my abilities, and my mind went from, *'Oh no, I'm screwed,'* to, *'Aiden, think about how much you studied for this test, it's going to be ok.'* That dose of confidence and calmness was exactly what I needed to move forward. I picked up my pencil and got started. To my surprise, the problems on my test started to feel easy, and I felt calm and relaxed when I handed my paper to the teacher at the end.

When it was all said and done, my biggest takeaway from this Deep Breathing Challenge was how much of an impact *pressure* can have on a person. There wasn't a single difference in how much information I knew for the test before and after I did the breathing, but there was a major difference in how much information I could access before and after my breathing. As an anxious person, I was amazed at how much calmer I felt, too.

Even to this day, I use this technique when I'm nervous because I now know that I can only control what I can control, which at test time, is how much pressure I am feeling. But it's not only at test time that this technique is helpful. Later in the school year, we were doing a presentation for English, and I felt so much stress and pressure because I knew I didn't finish the entire slideshow. Again, I wanted to just go home and hide in my sheets, but that wasn't an option, so I started to do the Deep Breathing Challenge again. And again, it helped to calm my nerves down, and I remembered some of the information I had failed to write down! I quickly wrote the details down on my notecard and actually got a decent grade on the presentation.

I didn't know this before, but stress and pressure really do stop your brain from remembering all the information it stores inside. Now I remind myself to let loose of the pressure I put on myself because I know that being calm, relaxed, and open-minded is the best way to do my best work on tests, assignments, and in presentations.

When My Mind Got Involved, My Body Followed

It sounded like a piece of cake. Just hold a plank for as long as you can. Easy. Or was it?

The next day, I woke up, got ready for school, hung out with some friends, came back, finished homework, had dinner, and so on. Just a normal day for a normal kid. As I was coming back from a hard session in taekwondo, it hit me - I had to finish my Plank Challenge.

I trudged up the stairs, dreading the fact I had to plank after all the exercise I had already done. Yes, I thought it would be easy at first, but thoughts can change in seconds. I grabbed my phone, set up a stopwatch, and started planking. I think about a minute passed when I realized that I didn't set a goal, and this made my planking kind of useless.

So, to at least make the challenge a little bit more enjoyable and challenging, I set a goal: 5:40. That might seem long, but planks had been part of my previous personal training routine, and my past record was 5:35. I told myself I could break that goal, and would break it, no matter what.

Well, maybe on another day it would be easier, but after all the kicking, running, and punching from taekwondo class, I was shaking all over and I collapsed seven seconds before my goal. I felt happy that I was able to complete the challenge even when my body felt like it was dying. But I had a lingering feeling of regret which whispered, '*dang, only seven more seconds and I could've reached my goal and beat my time.*'

I woke up on Tuesday, and well, it was just like Monday, but I had tutoring and soccer instead of taekwondo. It was a hot session on the soccer field, and I had pushed myself really hard. My body was killing me when I got back into the car and I was looking forward to a long, hot shower, a great dinner, and some time to rest before doing my homework.

Well, driving home, I remembered we had the Plank Challenge, and it suddenly felt like my soul had exited my body. Already, I was so tired, so hungry, and I wasn't in the best mood, but when I got home, I grudgingly pulled out my phone and set the stop-watch. Unlike the day before when I could almost beat my personal record, my body today was just dead, completely dead. After thirty seconds, it couldn't take anymore, and I dropped down. I felt a bit proud that I had done my best after the exhausting day I had, but at the same time, I failed again to meet or beat that 5:40 mark. This set a fire in me.

Throughout my entire Wednesday, I focused on wanting to beat the 5:40 mark at all costs. All day long, that was whispering to me in the back of my mind: 5:40, 5:40, 5:40. In fact, when I arrived home, the first thing I did was set up my stopwatch and get into position. I really wanted to break the mark.

I got my stopwatch, started it, and went right to work. But, every second felt like a year, and for whatever reason, the time was going slower than usual. Every time I checked the watch, it had only been like 5 or 6 seconds, and I thought to myself, "*it's over, I'm going to have to try again tomorrow.*" Then I said to myself, *'today's the only day I don't have any athletic activities going on, so today is my best chance to beat my record. Don't give up.'*

Even though it was hard, I kept pushing myself, looking for every ounce of strength in me to keep going. Then, I looked at the clock, and it said 5:37. I only had 3 seconds left. But, those three seconds felt like 3 centuries, and the time went by really, really slow. Like, it went 3…, 2…., 1……

When I finally crossed the 5:40 mark, I just collapsed into a heap on the floor and I couldn't stop smiling. It was like I had just fought an extremely long battle, and finally won. And that feeling lasted for the entire day, and I just felt really proud of myself.

Before this experience, I didn't realize how small things can have a large impact. I mean, to someone else, holding a plank may seem like a trivial thing but to me, it was a goal I set for myself. And it was a stretch goal that I had to push to achieve because it didn't come easy. I could have quit mid-way, but I didn't. And that not only made me proud, but also gave me a great amount of confidence, which changed something in me. I learned to pay attention to my hard days, and not try to do more hard things on those days. Another lesson from this challenge was to try things with more certainty that I could succeed. So, yes, this plank challenge did change me, and like Vince Lombardi said, "Winners never quit, and quitters never win."

In a Battle With Trapped Anger, Boxing Won

Ughhhhhh. I kept staring at it. 80 percent. 80 percent! That's the lowest biology grade I've received all year. Then I received my study questions back for the test the next day, and half my answers were wrong! Well, that did little to improve my mood. I had to go home and study basically everything again. At that moment, I just wanted to go home, lie down, and do nothing. But, that wasn't an option. So, here we go.

I arrived home and started my English project since I wanted to spend most of the evening studying. All was going well, and I thought to myself, *'Hey, at least one thing is going my way today!'* But, a crisis always occurs when least expected. Yup, my computer ran out of battery and I forgot to save my progress. All the energy and will to continue just left my body. I just threw myself on my bed, and thought to myself, *'Well, at least it can't get any worse.'*

I think I took a nap because I didn't feel like being awake and thinking about all the bad things that happened today. I don't know how long I was sleeping for, but I woke up to the sound of my dad yelling, "Aiden, you're late for practice!" Well, that got my heart pumping. I checked my phone and I only had 15 minutes before soccer practice started. I don't think I've ever gotten ready that quickly for anything. I rushed everything just so that I wouldn't be as late, and we arrived at practice about 10 minutes past the start time

After our drills, we were given a quick water break, but the next crisis hit me when I realized I rushed out of my house without taking any water, and it was a really hot day! So, I went around looking for a drinking fountain nearby, but they weren't working. I just told myself, *'It's ok, we just have an hour of practice left.'* But, as the minutes passed, I couldn't focus. When one of my teammates passed me the soccer ball to put it in the net, I couldn't see straight, and I just kicked the ball carelessly. Even though it was an empty net, I missed it by a mile.

After practice, I was just really hating the day I had. All that anger was piling up inside me, and I didn't think I could hold it in anymore. Luckily, I remembered a challenge we learned six weeks ago to practice air boxing to get out our frustrations or anger. I felt both of these emotions intensely so I thought, *'It helped me when I got a bad grade during the Air Boxing Challenge week, let me try it again now. What's the harm?'*

I got into my fighter's stance and put my hands into fists, by my face. I started to punch the air, but it wasn't really the air I was punching. Each punch was letting go of something that made me feel angry that day.

This punch was for my biology test grade.
This one for the study questions I got wrong.
This is for my alarm not waking me up.
This one for me being late for soccer.
One for me failing to bring water.
For my laptop battery dying.
For me, forgetting to save my work.
For missing the goal.

I punched over and over until I ran out of breath and my legs couldn't take the cardio shuffling anymore. Like the first time I used this technique nearly two months ago, it made me feel better.

I wouldn't think that each punch could improve my mood, but when I was done, I did feel much better.

If I didn't do any air boxing that night, I wouldn't have released all my anger and frustration, I wouldn't have been able to study for my next bio test with a fresh mind, and I would have hated my day. After visualizing each bad thing and then punching it away, I learned that it's important to let your frustration and negative feelings go. Anger is an emotion that can get trapped in your body, and it doesn't disappear until you let it out of your system. That's what air boxing did for me. It allowed anger to leave my body one punch at a time. And as anger left my body, I felt calm and ready to face whatever life was going to throw at me.

My Laziness Didn't Stand a Chance

It was a hot Monday in spring, and I had just got home from school. Like every other day, I had homework and assignments to do, but all I really felt like doing was lying on my bed and doing nothing for a few hours until I had to go to taekwondo. So, I decided that was what I was going to do - nothing. And for a few peaceful minutes, I was happy.

Suddenly, I remembered I had an English essay to start and finish that night. Well, that put me in a bad mood really quickly. I would normally do it after coming home from taekwondo and eating dinner, so I thought I would do that again today. I just didn't have the willpower to get out of bed, turn my computer on, and start writing.

Then, I remembered something else. Our IMPACT challenge started today, and this week's challenge was to use a quick technique to break our procrastination habits. The idea was that when we had a task we needed to do, we needed to start it within five seconds. In our meeting, we talked about our brains, and how we can think of something we should do, but if we wait more than five seconds, our brains will find excuses to put it off until another time. A five-second countdown encourages people to put their idea into action before their brain tells them not to bother doing it. Also, the countdown gives a small boost of energy and momentum to get started.

I figured there was no better time than now to test it out. So, I counted.

5..., 4..., 3..., 2..., 1....

Without resistance, I got up, and turned on my computer, opened my program, and started my English essay. I couldn't believe it. Normally, I would spend a lot of energy and brain power doodling off or wasting time for as long as possible, then when I actually started to write hours after I started, I would be tired, distracted, and out of good ideas. But once I started today, I had a much easier time writing than I usually do, my ideas were fresh, and I finished faster than usual. This was strange since the topic itself was a lot harder than the other ones we were assigned to in the past.

I wondered about this some more. Why would it be easier to write when the topic was harder? I figured my brain was still fresh and awake since it was in the afternoon, and not exhausted after taekwondo, dinner, and a few hours of nothingness. I saw that I was more efficient and made fewer mistakes when I was working earlier, even though all I wanted to do was rest in my bed until leaving for my taekwondo.

With the 5 second countdown, I was able to overcome my laziness because it gave me the motivation to start, especially when I really didn't feel like doing it in the first place. It also gave me a boost to just get it done so that it wasn't hanging over my head all night, reminding me every second I still had to start. The cherry on top for using this technique was that I got a lot more time in the evening to edit my first draft *and* have some relaxing free time without the feeling of dread that I had to finish an assignment because I had already got it done. That day, I understood Aristotle's words when he said, "Well, begun is half done."

An Interview With Author Aiden Jung Won Chang

Why did you join the IMPACT Project?

COVID had a large, negative impact on my life. I just ended up letting go a lot and got a lot lazier. Then, suddenly being thrown into high school and just school in general, that increase of pressure and stress overnight was pretty intense. I wanted to find a way to deal with all that.

I joined the IMPACT Project because I noticed my mental health, personal development, and leadership skills were all negatively affected by COVID. The biggest area I wanted to improve was managing stress, since, like everyone else, my stress level skyrocketed after being locked in for over one and a half years.

Also, I wanted to learn new strategies to manage expectations since I just started high school. High school is one of the most competitive stages of a person's life, and that creates immense pressure. I just really wanted to give myself the best chance of success and the biggest advantage.

Your stories showed us some really memorable moments about building resilience and gaining confidence, but I can imagine that some challenges transformed you but weren't your favorite ones. What would you say were your favorite challenges to do?

1. Make Your Bed & Tidy Up
2. Guided Meditation
3. Hold a Plank

Over the course of the program, I am sure you changed in many ways. What was your biggest takeaway and what do you now know about your ability to overcome hard things?

I now know when any hard thing comes my way, I'm going to persevere. My biggest takeaway is that the little things in life do make a difference, and they add up to create larger changes in life. If one of those little changes were different or never happened, life wouldn't be the same. Also, I learned that the process of how you do something is as important, if not more, than the outcome itself.

What advice would you give those who feel stressed, stuck, under pressure, or overwhelmed and don't know what to do?

1. Take a few moments and go away from the problem, clear your mind, then go back and think about the problem.

2. Write down what your problem is. Then, just write down a bunch of ways that might fix the problem.

Do you have any final words of wisdom?

Life is a one-way ticket, there's no going back. So, appreciate it while you can.

About the Author

Aiden Jung Won Chang

Have you heard this quote from legendary football coach Vince Lombardi? "Winners never quit, and quitters never win." If you were to describe Aiden Chang in one sentence, it would be that. He is a rising sophomore in high school in the United States. Being a student takes up most of his time. If he's not studying for the latest test or finishing his homework, he will be hanging out with friends, listening to music, mindlessly looking at the night sky, or just napping. His greatest enjoyment is watching or playing soccer, basketball, football, or baseball. He is part of a local soccer club and spends some weekends volunteering at a local food station. In the future, he wishes to provide what is best for his family and pursue a career in Korea.

Stress could be his biggest weakness, but he has learned a considerable amount about how to become a better person through the IMPACT Project and hopes that those lessons have translated well into the book. He also hopes the readers can appreciate the small things in life, just as he learned to do in this program.

CHAPTER 14

Insecurity Loses Its Hold On Me

By Yeonoo Jeong

Looking into the mirror, I see a reflection of myself. In my reflection, countless insecurities are mirrored back to me as I often focus on the negative aspects of my appearance. Even when I go on social media, I often see others having a seemingly better life: better grades, more friends, and such. I often see the worst parts of myself and dwell on my previous actions and experiences that were "embarrassing". I still can't sleep at night thinking back on the time I had a conversation with a stranger, only for them to be talking to someone else on a call. Or, that one time I waved back at a person who wasn't waving to me. Sometimes, even friendships tend to worry me as I don't know their true opinion of me. I begin thinking- does the other person even like me? It's a constant guessing game without an answer.

Through the IMPACT challenge, however, I was able to finally get an answer. I was given the challenge of "How Others See Me," which required me to ask a person what they admire about me. I was essentially able to directly ask someone the question, "What do you like about me?" At first, I was nervous about the awkwardness resulting from this interaction. My head filled up with the thoughts of *'What if they don't like me?'*, or, *'Will they think this is a weird thing to ask?'*

I decided to ask my question by text: "Hi! I'm asking this question for a project that I am involved in: what is one trait that you admire about me?" Contrary to my worries, the responses I received were very encouraging.

"You show dedication and persevere through the end."
"You have a good sense of humor and you're really funny."
"You make me smile."

After hearing these words, I felt my heart warming up, and I discovered a few things that were really important. First, their comments really helped me to calm my insecurities. Second, hearing what others appreciate about me taught me things about myself that I didn't know. For example, the constant worry about others' opinions now seemed futile.

It is often hard to know how much you mean to someone, especially friends, because we don't really talk about what we admire in each other. Hearing people's uplifting thoughts about me transformed my mindset to think more positively, and they helped me value myself more. Although I still think back on my embarrassing moments and insecurities, I am learning to let it go as people simply do not care about those things as much as you do yourself.

Embracing Waves of Peace and Calm

Imagine your body warming up by the bright sunlight while also feeling the cold breeze of the ocean cooling down your body, causing a perfect negative feedback loop. As you walk by the shore, the cool waves hit your feet. The air is filled with the sounds of waves washing up. Everything feels peaceful. This feels like a dream.

As a student who manages a busy schedule, I spend many days cramped in my room trying to juggle six AP classes and work on my extracurricular activities. With homework and big assignments piled up on my desk, clothes spread all over the floor, binders on the bookshelf, everything was clustered in my room. Especially during the pandemic, this small space became my everything. Whether it be taking classes or talking to friends, my whole life happened in my room. My blinds were often shut, and I was left with a yellow artificial light dimly illuminating my dark, gray room. The four walls started to enclose me, to suffocate me.

One week, we were asked to complete the "Nature Challenge," where we would go outside to be "one" with nature in silence, without any distractions.

One day, when I felt too overwhelmed and drained to do anything with my schoolwork, I decided to go to the beach. As the sun was setting, I sat in front of the water watching the sunset. Being out in nature without my phone, I was able to fully indulge and focus on my surroundings- the cool breeze, the sound of the waves washing up, the vibrant orange colors of the sky. I emptied my mind and didn't think about any of my current problems.

When the sun seemed to set completely, I looked at the time: an hour had passed. I felt completely vitalized and refreshed. My mind was clear. Physically being outside in an environment that I usually do not indulge myself in, I felt renewed.

By doing "nothing," I was able to recover from my lack of motivation and overwhelming stress and emotions. I realized that being in nature doesn't have to be at a significant location- it could be a park nearby, a backyard, or anywhere outside, as long as we are away from technology and our hectic lives. In the digital age, people tend to stay away from nature and forget that there is another world nearby. The world around is so vast and accessible to all. Even the action of stepping out of your room or house to feel the breeze can truly help you- so use it to your advantage!

Finding Gratitude on the Day My Car Was Scratched

I was having a great day. I had been craving brownies all day so I went to the store to buy a mix to make some at home. When I came back to the parking lot with my bag, I saw a huge scratch with yellow paint residue on my white car. My whole mood shifted and I started to panic. It had been only 3 months since I got my license and the third time my parents let me drive alone. This was terrible!

Being upset stayed with me all day. As I dozed away to sleep in my bed, my negative thoughts filled my head even more.

Was it my fault?
Should I have done something different?
Why do I have to pay for damage that someone else did?

Suddenly, I remembered our daily challenge, the one I hadn't completed yet. Creating a gratitude list. Seriously? This was going to be the hardest challenge for me, considering my situation. How could I possibly be grateful when all these bad things happened to me? I had to push the negative thoughts away and find things I could be grateful for: hanging out with my friends, getting a good grade on a test, and other ones like these.

Funny thing about the human mind is that it stores various things, but we have no clue *why*. I suddenly remembered a phenomenon from an educational comic book my parents made me re-read when I was eight: *negativity bias*. Human minds often display negativity bias, focusing more on the negative aspects of something, rather than the positives. Even looking at news stories or celebrity gossip, 90 percent of them are negative. The negative news is what catches people's attention, while the positive news praising a person gets overshadowed. Some may argue that this is how people evolved to be because focusing on the negative things kept us safe, on guard for other dangers.

As I thought about this, I asked myself, 'On a bad day, how many 'bad things' actually happened contrary to the 'good things?' One bad thing can completely destroy someone's day, overshadowing many good things that happened on the same day. The reality is the good things that happen are easily forgotten. So, how do we change our negativity bias?

Creating a gratitude list can help us overcome this habit. For me, finishing off the day with what I am grateful for reversed my current mood. I noticed that the negative aspects of my day were being overshadowed by the positive things that happened. The act of finding my pencil, opening up my journal, and thinking of the good things that happened to me helped me be more appreciative of my surroundings. Whether it was something as small as, '*my ramen tasted so good*,' or '*my friends were so funny today*,' I still thought of the positive things I don't normally take the time to appreciate. I tried to look for things to be grateful for and realized how I am taking many things for granted. Ending the day on a positive note made me appreciate my surroundings more.

Even though I was more appreciative and grateful, I still had to tell my parents about the big yellow scratch on my car. I was really nervous. Thankfully, when I told them, they were encouraging, they comforted me, and they reassured me that it was not my fault. That day, I realized that I was able to open up to them and rely on them for support, I knew for sure that they were on my side. Through this experience, I learned more about their love for me and to appreciate them more. Something else I was grateful for!

Now, although I still catch myself thinking back on the negative things that happened during my day, I don't push them away. Rather, I ask, '*what takeaways or lessons can I learn from them to help me grow?*' And, small actions like creating a gratitude list at the end of the day helps me challenge my natural negativity bias, and view my day to be half full, instead of half empty.

When I Got Started, I Just Couldn't Stop

Just walking across my room without stepping on something was... quite a challenge. Clothes, homework from school, old papers, the list goes on. My bookshelf was full of old binders from middle school that I hadn't looked at in years. My room, which was supposed to be a sanctuary where I could relax from my busy life, was one of the main reasons why I felt unorganized and messy. I often watched "room tour" videos done by influencers where they shared what looked like 'the perfect room.' I always wished I could clean up my room and redecorate it completely like them, but I lacked the time and motivation to put those thoughts into action.

It wasn't that my room was unorganized. With all the papers piled up on my desk, clothes on the floor, and old binders stacking up, I would often lose focus and begin procrastinating. There were too many distractions around me physically and mentally.

Just as I was pondering about what to do about my chaotic room, we were given the "Decluttering Challenge." This challenge required me to declutter three things every night, but really, it acted as a catalyst for a bigger change. By throwing out three things I didn't need, it was actually really easy to continue the momentum of decluttering. And, I saw that it wasn't just a chore, but rather an opportunity to finally get started on reinventing my room, something I had been putting off for too long. Each day of the challenge, I didn't stop at removing three things, I decided to throw away things from each part of my room instead.

I finally decided to tackle the one big drawer in my closet, the one where I put everything, like childhood mementoes or toys from Happy Meal boxes. When I opened the deep, full drawer, I could see all the things I once considered important but have now forgotten. Squished into one corner was my teddy bear, the one I carried everywhere. I was overwhelmed with a sense of nostalgia, and I pulled it out and squeezed it tight, reliving all my memories with it. This teddy bear essentially watched me grow up, listened to me share my countless tales, and cuddled with me as I fell asleep at night.

Then I turned back to my drawer, and I picked up a stack of cards my classmates wrote to me in second grade as a going away present. I used to live in Korea, and then in second grade, my parents told me we were moving to the United States. Being so young at the time, my brain was excited as it focused on what was coming, rather than being sad about all the things I was leaving behind. Reading the individual cards, a smile spread across my face. In sloppy handwriting and with words spelled wrong, these cards were moments frozen in time from my old classmates writing about how much they'll miss me. I began to think about my second grade class, and wondered, '*do they still think about me?*'

After my reunion with some of my old belongings, I had a bigger insight that I should not dwell on the past. While it was nice to look back, I thought that maybe we hold onto everything from our past as a way to idealize how great things used to be. But we don't need to hold onto everything to remember the great moments from earlier in our life. Although I couldn't throw away the handmade cards or let go of my teddy bear, I did let go of many things that were nice memories but needed to stay in the past.

Once the weekly challenge was over, I had finally decluttered my entire room and filled two large trash bags. I didn't have to dread my room or be distracted by all the piles of paper all over my desk. Once my room had less things taking up space, and once everything was put away, I could start creating my dream room, just like the influencers I would always watch.

I began by decorating my blank walls. I quickly bought all the materials I needed, and all the décor I wanted, and got started. I hung posters from my favorite movies, and pictures of my favorite artists. I filled my room with things that I adored, and decorations that made me, me. I created a clean and organized sanctuary of comfort, warmth and peace for myself, and I loved being there.

It was only after I created this huge transformation in my room that I realized how much our environment can impact our mental state. Before the Decluttering Challenge, I lived and studied in a messy and stuffy room, and I was often distracted. I can't even count how many hours I spent procrastinating with my piles of papers or looking for things I had misplaced. Without a doubt, studying in a clean room helped me focus more and procrastinate less. As a teenager, the only part of the house that I can control is my room. Although it took me about two years to declutter, clean, organize, and redecorate my entire room, it was truly worth it. It may not be easy to start, but every step in life begins with the decision to begin, even if you begin with something small.

An Interview With Author Yeonoo Jeong

Why did you join the IMPACT Project?

I joined the IMPACT Project in order to help find ways to help improve the mental health of people. In today's world, levels of anxiety are through the roof. This applies to me as well, as I often experience anxiety, stress, and overwhelm. The anxious thoughts collect themselves over time and accumulate into a negative cycle of anxiety. Whether the root of the problem is minor or monumental, it still causes stress or disruption in my life. If any of these mental health challenges in the IMPACT Project could help relieve some of the tension, I wanted to test these out for myself.

Your stories showed us some really memorable moments about building resilience and gaining confidence, but I can imagine that some challenges transformed you but weren't your favorite ones. What would you say were your favorite challenges to do?

1. How Others See Me
2. Be in Nature
3. Gratitude List

Over the course of the program, I am sure you changed in many ways. What were some strategies that really helped you learn more about yourself and your strengths? And how do you think you have developed in your personal growth over the past 5 months?

I changed in many ways, that's true. For example, I was able to learn more about myself through the "How Others See Me" Challenge. Directly hearing the positive things people like about me helped me realize that I am liked by people. This changed my perspective to see the good things about myself, helping with self-confidence.

Over the past five months, I learned how to manage stress and overwhelm better than I did previously. Before, I wasn't aware of what to do, but now I try out various methods to help me feel better. I feel more organized in managing my emotions, through various activities, such as throwing away old things, creating a gratitude list, etc.

What advice would you give those who feel stressed, stuck, under pressure, or overwhelmed and don't know what to do?

First, start with something simple. Even a minute of deep breathing can help relieve that tension and stress. Deep breathing is easy to initiate and can be done under any circumstances. If something with a stronger effect is needed, step outside. It can be a park nearby or the beach, just clear up your mind and don't think about anything. Sit out in nature and try to focus on things outside, while activating your five senses- how the wind feels on your skin, how vibrant the sunset is, and how the birds sound. Don't think about your problems and just try to clear your mind. After you calm down, now, go back to the problem. This little exercise might help you think more rationally, not solely based on your emotions.

Do you have any final words of wisdom?

Do not dwell on the past, especially on embarrassing moments. Not a lot of people remember it as much as you do.

About the Author

Yeonoo Jeong

Yeonoo Jeong is a senior in high school, and now a co-author of this book. She has lived in three different countries- England, Korea, and the United States. Moving around a lot made her think she was introverted, but as she settled in California and matured in her teen years, she realized she is more social than she thought.

She is fluent in English and Korean and can speak and write a bit of Spanish. She is the president/founder of several volunteer organizations that serve the community in the local sphere- volunteering in homeless shelters, packing hygiene products for the women's shelter, cleaning up parks- you name it, Yeonoo is happy to jump in to help.

When she's away from school and extracurriculars, she loves reading books, watching shows, listening to music, and hanging out with friends. In college, she is planning on majoring in psychology- a passion of hers.

Although she may be scared at first, she loves trying out new things and overcoming her fears, such as zip lining or riding a roller coaster.

CHAPTER 15

My Phone or Me. Who Was Really in Control?

By Faith Kim

During week 12, our challenge was to unplug before bed. When I was listening to the instructions for this challenge, I sat straight up in my chair and my eyes grew wide in utter shock because I honestly did not know if I could get through this challenge. Going on my phone right before bed was embedded into my routine.

On the first night, I turned off my phone, and as I trudged down my stairs, I groaned knowing I wouldn't have anything to do throughout the night. I reluctantly plugged it into the charger in my kitchen and ran back upstairs so I wouldn't be tempted to go back and touch it. My temptation kept growing, but I managed to stay disciplined because I believed there would be a great reward the next morning. Ever since I was a little girl, my mom would always tell me to put my iPad away before bed because the blue light would affect my ability to sleep. She said if I was able to withstand at least half an hour at night without it, I would feel more refreshed in the morning. When I was younger, I could never last that long, so I was hopeful to see if I would feel better by being screen-free before bed now that I was older.

As I lay in bed that first night, I tossed and turned. No matter how hard I tried to squeeze my eyes shut and sleep, they wouldn't stay closed. I could not remember how to fall asleep. The next morning, I experienced a rare moment that I have not encountered in ages; I woke up and things felt different. First, the sun was shining brightly into my room, and when I took a deep awakening breath, I could smell the clean crisp air outside my window. As I exhaled, all the overwhelming thoughts that normally make me feel rushed in the morning weren't there.

At first, I refused to believe that such drastic improvements in my attitude and mindset resulted solely from putting my phone aside just 30 minutes before bed. But, after a few screen-free nights and calm, relaxed mornings, I couldn't deny how much better I felt.

Even though this challenge was one of the hardest challenges I had done throughout this entire project, I strongly believe that this one had the most positive impact on my mental and physical well-being. To give you some encouragement, I can proudly say that even after many weeks have passed since this challenge was first given, I still continue to put my phone away 30 minutes before bed every night and in return, I enjoy all the benefits from it, like better sleep and more energy the next day.

From this challenge, I was able to realize that getting a good night's rest is extremely crucial to my mental health as well as my physical health. When I slept well, I was in a better mood the next day, and my overall attitude was more positive. I was also less resistant to doing some tedious activities like practicing piano or cracking open my SAT study book. As a high school student juggling sports, vigorous classes, maintaining relationships, and volunteering for causes I care about, my mood and energy play a big part in my motivation and success. All I had to do was put away my phone and go to bed earlier to feel better - physically and mentally. And, I finally felt like I was in control of using my phone, not my phone being in control of me.

Weightlifting: When the Heaviest Thing Isn't the Plates

My shoes hit the treadmill at a steady, consistent rate as I ran at my natural running pace. A thin layer of sweat developed on top of my forehead and my breathing became heavier and heavier. I was so lost in my music, I ended up running for thirty minutes, forgetting the original objective of the challenge: doing an aerobic exercise for 1 to 2 minutes. The music made me feel free from my thoughts, and even though running was tiring, it felt as if many of my constant worries about school and life just slipped away with every step.

It is well known that exercise keeps the body and mind healthy and strong. But sometimes I feel discouraged and disappointed in myself after working out. I love to go to the gym to lift weights three or four times a week. As I lift, I want to see some sort of progress in how much I lift each time. Sometimes I would fail to reach my targeted goal of how much I could lift, and I would feel extremely upset because I wasn't able to improve my strength that day. Intellectually, I know building muscle doesn't happen after any single gym day, but in my heart, I felt like I had let myself down. During this challenge I realized that I had been using the gym as my coping mechanism to manage my school and life pressure. However, I was also using my performance to judge myself, often quite harshly.

When we were first told about this challenge in our weekly meeting, I questioned how this activity could correlate to a positive mindset. As I was listening to the instructions, I was remembering all the times I felt worse after I went to the gym, all the days I didn't meet my targets, lift heavier weights, or see any progress. To get the most from this challenge, I had to do something different than lifting weights. I decided not to go to the gym that week and focus more on aerobic exercise.

Every day after my run, I paid attention to how I was feeling. I slowly realized that doing daily aerobic exercise increased my energy and boosted my mood. For example, my daily three-hour post-weightlifting-workout-naps weren't necessary anymore, and I found myself spending more time outside of my room and having longer conversations with my family.

During this challenge week, I was also able to reflect on the pressure I put on myself in my weightlifting. I realized that I was always disappointed with myself because I was trying to see big improvements every day, and I was pushing myself too hard to get there. Plus, I never gave myself time to rest or recover, or do other activities that used my muscles differently, like aerobic exercise. By deciding to run every day for this challenge, I noticed that I could do things differently to have even better physical and mental health, and celebrate all the strength I had built up over the past few years. I learned that exercise does keep the body and mind strong, but if we push too hard, we can lose some of the benefits of creating a positive mindset, and we can add even more pressure on ourselves. After this challenge, I know even more clearly how a positive mindset contributes to a healthy mental health.

Tidy Your Room, Tidy Your Life

My morning always starts off with a loud bbbeeeepp beeeeeeepppp. My alarm woke me up at 7:00 am by blaring right next to my ear. I shut off my alarm and slowly opened my eyes, gazing at my ceiling. I reluctantly pulled myself out of bed and trudged into my bathroom. I had to walk over my t-shirts and socks that I had left sprawled out on the floor. "*What a mess,*" I thought, and I walked right around it to get ready for my day.

I dreaded the long day ahead of me as I ran through (what felt like) a million things to do on my mental to-do list. Even though I hadn't completed anything yet, I felt drained and fatigued. I felt this way every day before tackling the "Make your bed in the morning, tidy up in the evening" challenge.

At first, I was hesitant about doing what I thought were extra chores every day. Plus, I didn't see how these challenges would have any effect on my mental health. Nevertheless, I organized my sheets, arranged my pillows, and tucked the corners of my blanket into my bed. I carefully stepped back and admired my work.

Immediately, I felt a sense of accomplishment, and I felt calm and collected. This one small task gave me the encouragement to check off almost every single task on my to-do list throughout the day.

The last task on my list that day was to tidy up my room. I stood in the doorway of my room and stared in disgust at how messy it was: textbooks, notebooks, and pencils were piled up on my desk, and my clothes were sprawled across the floor everywhere. The only thing that made me smile was my nice and neat bed from this morning. My pillow was fluffed, my stuffed animals were organized, and the corners of my sheets were nicely tucked.

'If a clean bed can make me feel such accomplishment, imagine how a clean room would feel?'

I groaned as I squatted down to pick up the t-shirt I would normally walk over, and put it back into my closet. I put my socks in my hamper and I tackled the mess on my desk. Cleaning my room seemed like such a backbreaking thing to do, but in spite of that, I committed to this challenge and in return, I felt fulfilled knowing that the next morning I would be rewarded with a completely clean room.

As I continued doing this challenge throughout the week, I was able to see how much of a significant effect this had on me mentally. Yes, all I was really doing was making my bed and tidying up my room. However, to me, I felt more put together and organized because I was able to walk into a clean room after a long and crazy day at school and feel relaxed, not even more stressed.

To me, the objective of this challenge was to tidy up our lifestyles and take control of how we manage our time and environment. For example, at first, making my bed was such a tedious task, but now it is something incorporated into my daily routine which shows that other long-term habits can be formed. I will be honest with you; it will take a huge amount of effort and commitment, but if you can stick with it, you will have a sense of accomplishment too. By building habits using small simple tasks like making our bed and tidying our room, we can make substantial progress in our lives. This is important for having a healthy, well-balanced life with a space that brings calm energy and a happy mindset so we can take care of our mental health.

Bugs and Lizards and Dirt, Oh My!

My school is an outdoor school, so most of my time is spent outside. Plus, I have swim practice every day at an outdoor pool. So, when I first heard about this week's challenge to Be in Nature, I thought to myself, "How could this challenge be any different than how I spend the majority of my day anyways?"

To experience the full effect of this challenge, I decided to do something that was completely different than what I normally do outside, so I decided to take on gardening. By doing gardening, I would really be able to get my hands dirty and *experience* nature instead of simply being *in it*.

As I stepped out into my backyard, I noticed some things right away. The birds were chirping loudly as they sat on top of their little birdhouse in the tree, and the sun was shining brightly, warming up the ground under my feet.

As I began working, I felt a wave of nausea when I looked around; within reach, I could touch two things I dreaded the most: bugs and lizards. Even though it wasn't on me, knowing a lizard was within my reach made me have tingling sensations running down my back. On top of that, ants were actually crawling on my legs. I bravely brushed them off and kept focus on working in the garden.

The warm feeling of the sun on my back felt so nice because lately, I had been spending a lot of time indoors either doing homework, studying, or scrolling endlessly on social media apps. Being in my room started to be stressful and draining because there is always something to get done. My mind was flooded with millions of thoughts, most of them reminders about what I need to do.

'Did I really finish all my homework?'
'Did I forget there was a test tomorrow?'
'Am I actually prepared for my swim meet tomorrow?'

Outside was different. As I began planting seeds and picking the strong minty-scented perilla leaves, the anxious thoughts that lingered in the back of my head slowly faded away. My only thought was to make sure I picked the leaves ever so carefully so they wouldn't rip or tear, especially since they were going to be used in a very important dish for our dinner. I guess it wouldn't matter too much if the leaves were ripped, but the refreshing minty crunch that bursts in your mouth as you bite won't happen the same way if the shape is not intact. I was very careful.

One requirement of our weekly challenge was to be in nature, and another requirement was to be off our devices. I was so concentrated on gardening, the thought of touching my phone didn't come into my mind once. Normally, if my phone is within my reach, I feel very restless because I want to check my school apps, social media, and emails all the time. However, the fact that I didn't need to go on my phone because I was so present in my gardening made me realize there are so many other things to do in life that being on my phone prevents me from doing, such as interacting with nature like I was doing that afternoon. Once this realization entered my mind, I couldn't help but notice a smile forming on my face.

After a couple of hours, sweat was rolling down my face, my back was sore, and my knees were throbbing. Even through all this, I continued to garden until I was finished, and I felt so accomplished.

You may be wondering how this challenge impacted me personally. You might say that since I spent so much time outside on a daily basis, this activity wouldn't be that different. That was exactly what I was thinking as well. I don't think it was just that I was outside though; I think it was impactful because it was something new and different. Plus, gardening helped me be present in the moment, paying attention because I wanted to pick the best leaves for our dinner.

Being in nature this way was also helpful to me because I was able to take my mind off all the stress and worries and pressure to do schoolwork that I usually carry within me, and it allowed me to feel at peace for a couple of hours. Especially because my hands were in the dirt and pushing away the ants on my legs, I wasn't even thinking about my phone, I was only thinking about being in my garden. Having a day where I could really unplug and work outside under the warm sun was a good way to recollect myself.

An Interview With Author Faith Kim

Why did you join the IMPACT Project?

Before I began the IMPACT Project, I was an extremely heavy procrastinator and often lost motivation to do my homework and go to my swim and water polo practices every day. Usually, I put a smile on my face and acted as if I was handling everything in my life *just fine.*

However, I was always tired and often wanted to lay in my bed and do absolutely nothing. I needed to do things differently, so I was inspired to start the challenges and pay close attention to how they affected me emotionally, physically, and mentally. After doing these challenges, I would take my experiences and see if I could apply any of these to my life on a daily basis to improve my habits.

Personally, I wanted to learn new strategies that would help me manage stress, overwhelm, and pressure because I am now entering the hardest year of high school: junior year. If my mindset is not in a good place even before I've started 11th grade, I honestly do not think that I can make it through the year maintaining a healthy mental state.

So, with this project, I hoped to learn how to manage my stress and fix my habits and mental health so that I am able to maintain a positive and healthy mindset throughout the year and continue to apply these practices hopefully for the rest of my life.

Your stories showed us some really memorable moments about building resilience and gaining confidence, but I can imagine that some challenges transformed you but weren't your favorite ones. What would you say were your favorite challenges to do?

1. Be in Nature
2. Stretching Yoga
3. Deep Breathing

Over the course of the program, I am sure you changed in many ways. What is your biggest takeaway from participating in the IMPACT Project?

I learned that mental health is extremely important to my well-being because essentially, my mentality is what will allow me to do everything that I do.

What advice would you give those who feel stressed, stuck, under pressure, or overwhelmed and don't know what to do?

Feeling stressed, overwhelmed, stuck, or under pressure is a very common feeling for everyone so I hope that you know you are not alone. After a long day at school or work, you might feel that it won't get any better, but this is when you need to take care of yourself once in a while. On these stressful nights, something I recommend is to put all your work aside for a couple of hours and do something for yourself. It can be something as simple as taking a nap or treating yourself to your favorite food. I know that dropping your mental to-do list might be a bit nerve-wracking, especially for those who overthink or bury themselves in work, however a break from your responsibilities once in a while won't do any harm, and if anything, it'll increase your desire to work harder because of the enjoyable break you took for yourself.

Another thing you can do while feeling stressed is to simply take a couple of deep breaths in and out. Essentially this is a quick, easy and extremely effective activity to do right before doing anything that could make you a bit nervous such as taking an important test or going into an important interview. Speaking from personal experience, I took deep breaths in my car right before walking into my school and it was so helpful, especially because my hardest class was my first class of the day. Taking deep breaths and letting it out really helped me clear my mind even though my responsibilities were still there. To me, it really felt as if I was breathing out my worries as I was exhaling and I noticed that it significantly improved my mental well-being throughout the week.

Do you have any final words of wisdom?

Always remember to prioritize your mental health because your mental health is what creates your mindset and how you live your life.

About the Author

Faith Kim

Faith Kim is a high school student going into her junior year. At her high school, she is part of the varsity water polo and swim team. She also volunteers for a hospital in Downey and works at an aquatics center as a swim instructor for children. Faith enjoys running in nature, going to the gym, playing the piano, and spending time with her friends and family. In the future, she wants to further her education by going to college in order to step into the medical field so she can help others around her.

Faith is someone determined to educate herself about mental health since it is an essential aspect of a successful life. Over the past months, Faith has worked hard to complete many different challenges given by the IMPACT Project to see if they had any positive effects on her time management skills and procrastination. She has seen a vast difference in her habits recently in terms of procrastinating less and learning to manage her time better. She strongly recommends others to try these challenges too!

CHAPTER 16

When the Whole Game Rests On Your Shoulders

By Daniel Kwon

I sat at my desk, dreadfully thinking of things to write on my joy list, with sighs of annoyance. This was the third day we had to write down anything that made us feel joyful or happy. But each day I did it, I didn't feel like it had any effect. On top of that, my day was going horribly because I had to take three tests at school, and we lost our baseball game.

Anxiety and overwhelming thoughts filled my head, distracting me from thinking of anything that made me joyful. However, I knew that I could not just let my day end like this, so I said to myself, *'My day could not get any worse, so why not just try this again and hope it can help.'*

I picked up the pencil once again and started writing down simple and easy things that I knew made me joyful: friends and family, playing soccer and baseball, going on vacation, winning championships, and sleeping. Once again, I thought to myself that this exercise will not affect me, and it was just a waste of time. When I was done, I sat there staring at my list feeling frustrated that I made a list for nothing. I looked at each word and thought about how they made me feel joyful, until "winning championships" caught my eye. I lingered for a moment, then decided it was useless and I left my room for some water.

On the way to the kitchen, the words 'winning championships' stuck with me. Then I looked up and something amazing caught my attention: my trophy case. I walked over to it and saw my largest trophy in the center, which our team won for winning a widely known baseball tournament. At that exact moment, a memory popped up in my head.

Suddenly, I was back in that championship game.

My team was down 3-2 in the last inning. It was almost certain we were going to lose. We had our last chance to hit, and at that moment we had 2 outs.

My teammate went to bat, and I was on deck to go next. To be honest, I knew that I always fumbled the game in game-winning moments or messed up when the game was on the line, so I silently wished my teammate would strike out so that the game would end. I did not want to be the player to be the last one out, costing us the game.

In the midst of those thoughts, the pitcher wound up his arm and threw the ball, and as soon as I looked up, I heard a loud ping; I saw a glimpse of the ball skyrocket into the air and watched the outfielders sprint as they turned their backs to home plate. The ball hit the fence as he made it safely to second base.

I stood there watching it all unfold, my eyes in disbelief. Immediately, I started shivering and trembling. Sweat started dripping all over my face as I felt absolute nervousness. I knew if I messed this up and became the last out, with the game on the line, I would embarrass myself and my team and I would take all of the blame for losing the game. Already doubting myself, I dreadfully walked out of the dugout towards home plate.

It wasn't a quiet walk, though. People were cheering loudly, and others were shouting left and right. This was it. It was up to me whether my team would take the trophy, or to go home empty-handed. I looked back towards the dugout. My teammates jumped up and down in excitement as my coach told me to relax in the batter's box.

I took a deep breath and proceeded to step into position. Adrenaline rushed inside of me, and I was trying to steady my hands around the bat. With each breath, I told myself *'anything is possible, just don't give up,'* and *'I am going to get a hit right now.'*

The pitcher threw the ball.
Strike one.
Strike two.
Ball one.
Ball two.

I had never felt more nervous in my life. My whole body was trembling and quivering, and I just wished at that moment that I could have been at home or anywhere else instead of in the batter's box.

Sweat was dripping into my eyes, and my nervousness was skyrocketing. The next ball would determine the outcome of the whole tournament, and it was all on me. I glanced over at the trophy, placed right on the table behind the backstop, which filled me with confidence.

The pitcher stared at me, then threw the ball. I felt myself freely swinging the bat with all my strength. I watched the outfielders turning and running backwards, then in disbelief, I saw the ball flying way past their heads, barely bouncing before the fence. My teammates were yelling at me to run, so I dropped the bat, and I ran as fast as I could.

I flew through the bases.

First base.
Second base.
Third base.

I wiped sweat and dust from my face, and I saw my coach signaling me to go all the way to home plate. With all the strength

I had left, I reached out and dove into home plate. At the same time, I saw the catcher with the ball in his glove, tagging me as I reached home plate.

Everybody stopped right away and looked to the umpire. It took a moment but felt like forever, and then he yelled my most favorite word in all of sports: *safe*.

We had won the championship! I jumped off the ground and raced towards my teammates, as they started to swarm me in celebration. That day, I learned to never give up, and to always be confident in myself – no matter how the game is going or how nervous I feel.

I got my glass of water and returned to my room. I saw my joy list on my desk, but instead of it having no impact at all, I was grateful because it helped me remember one of the greatest moments of joy in my life. All of the anxiety, frustration, and overwhelm from my day had washed away, and I saw that creating a joy list wasn't just putting items on a paper but reliving the joy they brought to your life.

How To Bend When You Are Stiff as a Stick

I sat on my hardwood floor, tangled up in pain, grunting and groaning every second. Putting myself into these yoga positions was not too difficult but holding them for a few seconds felt like an eternity. After the timer went off for the yoga stretch to come to an end, I was filled with relief and relaxation. However, this sensation did not last for long as the next yoga stretch turned out to be even more difficult. I pushed through the last stretch, complaining quietly, yet compelling myself to continue the challenge. I heard the timer go off one last time, letting me know this challenge is finally over. I was relieved until I realized that I have to do this for five more days straight.

Before I started the Yoga Stretching Challenge, I knew I was stiff as a stick. I was worried that doing the yoga stretches would be more painful than beneficial. However, I committed to do it every day for a week, so each day, I stepped out of my comfort zone to finish the challenge, trying to endure the struggles of even reaching my toes.

After every session, I saw improvements in several different areas of the exercises: the level of stretches increased, I was able to go deeper in the stretch, and I experienced less pain during the stretches.

The most surprising aspect was how this challenge even improved my performance in soccer and baseball, my two current sports. As an athlete, especially as a soccer player, my legs are usually very tight; stretching is not something we do very often as a team, and I had almost never done it on my own. Because of this, when I started the yoga challenge, my ability to do any of the poses well was limited, but by the end of the week, I was able to finally touch my toes.

On top of that, I noticed that just one week of yoga and stretching prevented me from having injuries in practices and games. This is really important to a player because an injury can keep you out of the game for weeks, or longer.

I did not believe it would make a difference for me, but stretching is now part of my daily routine. I continuously see improvements in my flexibility, endurance, and performance in my sports. Although in the beginning, it was a struggle for me, I kept going and realized that my feelings of accomplishment drove me to try even harder the next day.

Each day I felt that my motivation grew, and I learned that even if it's hard at first, never give up.

Leave Your Troubles on the Trails

I had gone walking in the park or hiking before, but often I was on my phone or listening to music because I didn't want to be bored out of my mind. Being in nature was almost useless and worthless as I would be so focused on my phone, I wouldn't notice any of the scenery around me. Plus, being on my phone was what I normally did at school and at home, so what difference would being outside really make?

This week's challenge was to be in nature and be off our devices. I didn't think I was going to like this activity, but I did it anyway.

When I got to the trail, I was looking everywhere but straight ahead. I looked left and right, up and down. Without my phone, I saw large pine and oak trees swaying in the breeze, and dreamy clouds steadily floating by. Without my music, I could hear birds chirping and the sound of wind flowing through the leaves and branches. I noticed that as I focused my full attention on nature, I realized more of the details of the things around me: the colors, the shapes, the patterns.

I also noticed being outside without any distractions helped me remove some of the negative feelings that were impacting my mental health. Stress from school, an overwhelming workload, and a constant busy schedule were just some of the roots of the things that were holding me down and burdening me. I really felt like the weight of all these things were sitting on my shoulders, pushing me down.

As I was thinking about it, some of the things pushing me down were small and unimportant and didn't need to be on my mind all the time. When I looked around on my hike at the giant trees and sprawling bushes, I realized nothing in my life compared to the immense level of nature all around me. Slowly, I felt the pressure and anxiety I felt before just fade away, allowing me to rest my mind for a little while.

During this moment, I also experienced the rare feeling of being free. I was free from everything I had to do, everything at home and at school, and it was just me and nature, one on one. As I hiked, I was free to think deeply and reflect upon myself, my mental health, and truly understand who I am. One thing I learned about myself is that instead of being anxious and worrying about my small, daily problems, I could use that time to help others; sometimes hardships and challenges in their life cause them to have negative mental health effects far worse than I experience in my life.

After this challenge, I started being in nature more often without being on my phone. Now I hike with my dog to a nature-lush trail every day, and I am free to reflect on things that happen in my day, such as my emotions, feelings, and thoughts; what causes those emotions, the mistakes I made and ways I can fix them, how I can grow from them, how my actions and thoughts impact others, and how they see me as a result of this, etc.

Being in nature is a free and essential tool to use when you are overwhelmed or stressed, as it sets your mind away from all of the negative, worldly distractions. Even focusing on nature on a walk in the park without your phone or distractions will allow you to feel refreshed and settled down from anxiety or depression, which gives hope for the future.

Managing the Mess Once and For All

"BEEP BEEP BEEP BEEP BEEP BEEP"

The horrendous, obnoxious sound of my alarm broke the silence in my room, and I knew it was time to wake up, but I felt like I was going to collapse if I got up at that moment. My head was throbbing from staying up until 2 AM to study for my test. My legs were killing me because of a two hour soccer conditioning practice yesterday after school. My arms were about to fall off because of the soreness from the baseball workout two days ago. With all this pain and suffering I felt before I even left my bed, I thought it was my time that God should call me to come to heaven.

Knowing that I did not want my mom trying to wake me up, I slowly stood up, like I was a zombie who had just risen from the grave.

Then, I remembered that this week's challenge had two parts. The first was to make our bed. I felt burdened with dread because I thought that this task was just time consuming and useless. I had rarely made my bed before and always left my room without fixing it. So, with the least amount of effort, I tossed my blanket over my bed and straightened it out without moving my arms too much.

However, as I saw that my bed was well made and clean, I felt a sense of accomplishment and motivation, which gave me a boost of energy.

The second part of the challenge was to tidy up at night. Even though my bed was perfect, my room was not. I had clothes on the bed and floor, extra blankets tossed and turned, and stuff everywhere. After I paid attention to how messy my room was when I got home from a long day, I noticed that it made me feel more stressed and overwhelmed, and even my mood would become worse.

Even though my parents told me all the time to make my bed and clean my room, I thought doing those tasks were too much of a hassle and ended up not doing them at all. However, being involved in the IMPACT Project meant that I had to complete both of these required challenges.

When I started my day by making my bed, I noticed so many more positive changes than when I did not make my bed. First, I felt accomplished after doing a productive task first thing in the morning, which motivated me to complete even more tasks throughout the day. Then when I consistently completed the tidying challenge at night, I noticed that I stopped procrastinating and ended up doing my laundry, folding my clothes, and tidying my desk. Even though I didn't want to do them, I noticed it made me feel better to have a clean room and a nice bed to get into at the end of a long day. When I had more time and more space in my room, I added some new activities to my nighttime routine, like doing yoga stretches and preparing for the next day. Even though at first it may seem like making your bed and cleaning your room is a hassle, you will feel better about yourself and more accomplished in your life.

An Interview With Author Daniel Kwon

Why did you join the IMPACT Project?

I wanted to participate in the IMPACT Project to spread knowledge and awareness about mental health. At first, I was oblivious and clueless about the importance of mental health, however, as I retained more knowledge about it, it seemed to me that it is very essential. I was eager to learn more about mental health and ways to deal with it as well. Also, I found that doing these challenges week by week improved my mental health in every way, whether it is helping me cope with stress, or even improving my self-esteem and confidence. On top of that, I found sharing my experiences and thoughts as well as hearing others' very interesting, as we do activities and challenges together as a group who are relatively in the same age group also doing these challenges with me.

With this knowledge I gained in the IMPACT Project, I hope to spread some hope and inspiration to others and inform others about the essential role that mental health plays in our lives.

Your stories showed us some really memorable moments about building resilience and gaining confidence, but I can imagine that some challenges transformed you but weren't your favorite ones. What would you say were your favorite challenges to do?

1. Be in Nature
2. Make Your Bed & Tidy Up
3. Air Boxing

Over the course of the program, I am sure you changed in many ways. What were some surprising things you realized about yourself over the first few months?

Some surprising things that I realized about myself over the first few months were that I found myself persevering and being determined to complete the challenges every day, even if they were difficult or something that I did not look forward to. Also, another thing that surprised me over the first few months was the great effects these challenges had on me. Even the simplest challenges such as deep breathing and making my bed had significant and substantial effects on me. For example, deep breathing helped me deal with overwhelm, which allowed me to push through difficult and stressful homework, most importantly, getting through the most rigorous time of the school year. I also found out a lot more about my habits and how mental health plays a significant role in my life. Just by doing these challenges and lessons each week, I started realizing my own emotions and mental health more often, as well as knowing how to deal with negative mental health.

What advice would you give those who feel stressed, stuck, under pressure, or overwhelmed and don't know what to do?

My advice for those who feel stressed, under pressure, or overwhelmed, is first of all take deep breaths and even try the box breathing challenge that we did. Next, step outside, and do your favorite outdoor activity, which could be taking a light jog around the neighborhood, playing with your dog, riding your bike, etc. Also, you could try any of the challenges we did, but personally, I felt that the Nature Challenge, Aerobic Exercise, and Deep Breathing Challenges were most effective for me when I felt stressed or overwhelmed.

Do you have any final words of wisdom?

Live every day like it's your last. Make every moment count. And always be the best person you can be.

About the Author

Daniel Kwon

Daniel Kwon is a rising junior attending high school in Orange County. He is intrigued to learn more about mental health and wants to help spread awareness about how important it is to one's wellness and happiness. At his high school, he participates in various activities such as varsity soccer and baseball, two sports he is passionate about playing. He is also a non-profit youth trainer for soccer and baseball players, and he uses the revenue to donate to local sports centers.

In his free time when he's not playing sports, he loves to be in nature, spend time with family and friends, and work out. As he was playing two sports, being involved in several extracurriculars, and managing schoolwork, Daniel sought to find solutions to handle his busy schedule. In the IMPACT Project, he noticed the most growth for him was in areas of time management and his ability to overcome overwhelm.

In the future, Daniel plans on going to college to pursue business and sports management.

CHAPTER 17

When Music Carries You Through

By Daniel Youn

One more second! Just one more!

Come on; you got this. Hold it for one last second!

On the first day of the Plank Challenge, I laid down on the hardwood floor and got into position. As I held my plank, I was groaning in pain, trying to stay balanced and motivating myself to hold on for one extra second. My room was completely silent, except for the noises I was making. Every second felt like an eternity. I quickly realized I wasn't going to get through six days of this.

The next day, I opened my music app and found my favorite song. Like yesterday, every second I held the pose was another second I could feel my body shaking. One part of my brain kept sending me a message: please stop! At the same time, the other part of my brain kept up with the music and the beat playing through my speakers. I wanted to quit, but the part of my brain that was focusing on the music was stronger. I really concentrated on every beat and every sound in the song and pushed away any thoughts about my physical strain and uncomfortableness.

On day three, I put my music on again. I started my plank while I was vibing and singing along with the lyrics to my favorite song. I was

162

doing great, but then my body wanted me to stop. I thought to myself, *'Come on, Daniel, don't give up. Let the music carry you to the one-minute mark. Make your goal.'* I kept watching the time. When I reached forty-five seconds, the pain in my arms and abs began to flow through my body like a tidal wave wrecking everything in its way.

My song was still playing so I told myself, *'Stop looking at the time and focus on the song. Hold on a bit longer.'* I squeezed my eyes shut and felt the music inside of me, flowing in my veins. When I opened my eyes, I was shocked to see that I had held my plank for ten seconds longer than I could yesterday.

Without any doubt, music made me stronger. I could not believe the power of the catchy melody and strong beat to help me push through to my big goal. Setting that new personal record in the Plank Challenge gave me immense satisfaction and achievement. But I learned something else as well: I could not live without music.

Music is my life's motivator, and it is always there for me when I feel anger, fear, sadness, disgust, surprise, anticipation, and joy. It seeps through my life quietly and calmly to the point where my life would be incomplete without music. I saw the power of music to help me through this IMPACT challenge, and I know I will always have music in my life; I discovered it is an undeniable and necessary factor that motivates me to live my best life.

Sprinting Through the Streets of Hollywood

Huff, Huff. As I burst out through the gate near Colfax Street after a long day at school, I began my daily journey back home. Luckily for me, this week's IMPACT challenge was to do an aerobic exercise, and I was ready to run. On my back was my gray Hershel backpack, which unfortunately weighed around fifteen pounds. My legs were heavy and tired from sitting at a desk for eight hours, and as usual, the temperature in California was hitting 90 degrees. It was scorching hot

I was out of breath from dashing through the side gate, but I kept heading toward North Hollywood Station. As I was running, every muscle was moving, expanding, and contracting to keep me moving forward. After about ten minutes, my shirt was completely soaked in sweat from the speed of my legs and the heat off the pavement, but it wasn't bad at all; I felt energized and motivated by the dopamine released while running. Two more blocks under the blistering sun, and I finally reached my final destination: North Hollywood Station.

When I slowly walked down the dark and gloomy stairs of the station, I realized that all the stress I felt all day had disappeared; I really felt fresh and new. I began to see that running was one of the best methods to escape stress and anxiety. Just like how running helped me reach North Hollywood Station to get me back home, it was also a way I could use to escape stressful situations and get me feeling centered again.

Before participating in the IMPACT challenge, I would walk my route with a frown, worrying about homework and other tasks to complete. However, running was the perfect aerobic exercise to help me clear my mind so I could become more productive and energized all night.

Working Smarter, Not Harder

One thing every high school student dislikes is tests, and AP tests are at an even higher level. During AP season, many high school students struggle, trying to do their best on their rigorous AP exams but worried their results will not bring them the positive outcome they want.

When I thought back to last year's AP season, I remember I was often confused about what to study and how to study. Plus, I was so overwhelmed and stressed about having so many units to cover, and never enough time to cover them all. The pressure was almost unbearable. This year was a bit different. Through the IMPACT challenges and our various training on time management, study skills, and the importance of utilizing our calendar, I had an easier time managing homework and improving my studying habits.

However, even with these new skills, I was feeling stressed in AP season because there was still a lot of pressure to do well on these exams, especially as a junior. For over a month, I spent hours every night solving problems in my AP prep books.

When we heard about our new weekly challenge, I was worried about how I would add a new daily task to my long list of things to do. We were given instructions to complete guided meditations and some links to get started. I went onto YouTube and searched for videos on guided meditation, and I saw there were thousands of different options. I had no idea which one was going to be helpful. Feeling confuzzled, I clicked the video with the most views.

I closed my eyes and listened to the narrator's calm voice. As I let go of my pencil, I relaxed briefly. The thought of doing work slowly faded away. The only thing on my mind was following the narrator's voice through the guided meditation. As I breathed in and out, I felt my blood get pumped out of the right atrium into the left atrium in my chest.

When the guided meditation ended, I noticed my heart was beating slower and I was in the zone where I could focus on preparing for the AP exam. That night, I studied without distractions, and felt clear about answering all my practice questions.

After participating in the Guided Meditation Challenge all week, and taking the AP exam, I felt like I was able to do everything I could to be successful. With the new study habits and time management skills, along with the guided meditation to stay calm and increase my concentration, I was confident about achieving my goals above and beyond. Even after AP season was over, using guided meditation videos to improve my focus also helped me become more productive so that I could finish my work faster. This was a great challenge for me to learn how to be more effective in preparing for exams; however, I know that I will continue to use it anytime I need to calm down, refocus my attention, and center myself.

True Friends Always See the Real You

As an introvert, talking to new people and reaching out is always tricky. I have always been insecure about how I looked, how I dressed, how I spoke, and who I was. I feared people might not like me just because I was me.

Although I was born in the USA, I lived in South Korea for many years and was more exposed to Korean culture than American. Being unfamiliar with American culture, I was always scared about other people's perspectives on me. Plus, my accent and my looks made me hide my true self away from people I knew.

Before being part of the IMPACT challenge, I had no idea how other people viewed me, and I never had the opportunity to ask what they thought of me. Doing the *"How Others See Me"* Challenge changed my opinion of myself because in this challenge, I got to ask them how they see me and who they think I am.

On the first day of the challenge, I repeatedly opened and closed iMessage as I considered if I should even send the text message to my friends. I thought, *'What would they say?'* After pushing through my fear of reaching out, I managed to send the text. I told them I was working on a project and needed to ask people what they thought of me.

Before I received any responses, I expected to see words like *quiet, disinterested, and alienated* because I was always silent and tired in school. However, most of my friends responded that I was *genuine, kind, and passionate.* Hearing this response, I was astonished. My jaw was left open for a few minutes.

After I collected all the responses and reviewed them, I realized I don't need to be afraid of being myself in front of other people, and that my friends did in fact see the real me. The other realization I had was that no one will be accepted by all 7.7 billion people living on Earth; it only matters that we are accepted by our friends and people we want in our lives.

I'm grateful I found a group of friends who like me for my personality. With each other, we don't need to worry about how we look, dress, act, and talk. As I spend more time with them, we're building relationships with each other that feel really good, and I am thankful for our friendships.

An Interview With Author Daniel Youn

Why did you join the IMPACT Project?

At first, I questioned, *'How in the world is me participating in an 18-week challenge project going to change my life?'* I was very skeptical and unsure about participating in this project. However, as I began participating in the IMPACT challenges, I started to see changes in myself. From the challenges, I began to experience self-growth. Each week was a new learning opportunity and a chance for me to develop my leadership skills and personal growth. After learning how to manage stress and feeling overwhelmed, when I faced these situations again, I knew how to overcome these problems.

Your stories showed us some really memorable moments about building resilience and gaining confidence, but I can imagine that some challenges transformed you but weren't your favorite ones. What would you say were your favorite challenges to do?

1. Hold a Plank
2. Air Boxing
3. Aerobic Exercise

Over the course of the program, I am sure you changed in many ways. How would you describe yourself before and after the IMPACT Project?

Before the IMPACT Project, I had a lot of doubts about myself, especially doubts about my self-confidence. As an introvert, reaching out to people was the most fearful thing. However, through the IMPACT challenges, I saw myself grow and step out of my comfort zone to reach out to my family and friends. I became more confident and learned that I could do everything if I genuinely believed in myself.

What advice would you give those who feel stressed, stuck, under pressure, or overwhelmed and don't know what to do?

If you are feeling stressed and stuck, I advise you to try going on a walk or running on the sidewalk as fast as you can.

Try to do things you enjoy. Personally, I love to play and listen to music. Play your favorite song and try to forget about things that make you feel overwhelmed.

Lastly, you don't have to hold everything inside. Sometimes it is better to let things out, especially things that hurt you internally. Cry it out, scream, punch the air. You do not have to feel stressed about anything. Just be yourself.

Do you have any final words of wisdom?

We need to be grateful for everything we can see, eat, do, and experience since it may not be available to everyone.

About the Author

Daniel Youn

Daniel Youn is a rising senior who attends high school in north Hollywood. He is 18 years old and loves participating in various challenges and activities to test his limits. At his high school, he is part of multiple clubs like the Varsity Tennis Team, Science Olympiad, Cyberpatriot, and Math Club. In addition, he loves and believes that everything in life connects to music. With his passion for music, he learned how to play various instruments: piano, flute, cello, guitar, bass, and electric guitar. He is the co-president of the Music For Sharing non-profit organization and uses his talent to host performances at local hospitals.

Although he is an introvert, he loves to spend time outside with his close group of friends. He enjoys meeting new people but as someone who is timid, getting close to him might take some time, but once you do, you will see a different person! During his free time, he naps and plays basketball at a park nearby. When he goes to college, he is interested in studying computer science, data science, and psychology. After graduating college, he wants to start a startup or work as a computer programmer in a big-tech company.

Part IV

Chapter 18

Challenge Reflections

Our teens completed daily challenges and then wrote extensive reflections about their experience each weekend.

Below, you will find a selection of their insights, learnings, and experiences to get an up close and personal view into how each strategy worked for them, and how it made a difference in their lives.

Deep Breathing

I use this strategy in my everyday life to relax, recollect my thoughts, and just cool down. After a long day of work or studying, this helps me rest my mind and fall asleep faster.

Deep breathing helped so many times, like when I was taking a test and during my sports games. It helped me calm my anxiety and nervousness, and boosted my confidence so I actually performed better.

I felt that it helped eliminate my overwhelm and negative thoughts that were constantly building up during the day. It was helpful despite how fast and easy it is to do.

At first I wasn't sure if breathing a couple of times would really make me feel any better but after trying it for a week, I found it to be very helpful. It calmed me down and helped me mentally get ready for things I had to do.

Stretching Yoga

The challenge was effective physically and mentally; it released the stress and tension in my body, and it also helped clear my mind and put me at ease emotionally.

It is an easy activity that helped me feel more awake and refreshed. It was a nice transition to do after waking up to stretch and "warm up" my body.

It loosened up any physical pains or soreness and made me feel free from the body pain that was caused by school stress, tests, etc.

It felt stress-relieving to stretch in the morning, especially because my back is quite stiff from sleeping.

Compliment Someone

I love complimenting others. It's a way to share positivity in a world that can be very judgmental and harsh. It encourages us to interact with others and feel more connected.

It's a good way to cheer someone up when they're feeling down; one compliment can really change their day.

Whether it was appreciating my hard-working mom or telling my brother how beautiful he plays the piano, complimenting others is easy and makes someone's day.

When I complimented my friend about his high test score, he felt good and it made me feel good as well. That's when I thought about the quote "happiness is contagious".

Create Your Joy List

I think that creating a Joy List made me more appreciative of smaller things in life that in the past, I would have overlooked. There are often good things that happen that I forget about. However, creating this joy List made me feel more appreciative.

When I went back and looked at my Joy List, I automatically felt better. I ended my day with happy memories and went to sleep peacefully with a smile.

I immediately wrote down the joyful memory to not forget it. So, when I'm facing hard times or if I am not feeling happy lately, the list will always be there to remind me of each fun memory.

I went for a run on a trail and the flowers were in bloom. There were yellow, purple, and white flowers growing everywhere. It was so beautiful and brought me so much joy, I had to write it down as soon as I got home.

Make Your Bed & Tidy Up

My favorite challenge was making my bed because it was the most impactful. It helped me realize how the small things in life make a huge impact on our mental health. Just the simple task of making my bed made me feel good first thing in the morning since I had a feeling of accomplishment.

Some mornings, it felt like a drag to fluff up the blankets. After all, I was going to be ruining it at night anyway, so what's the point? But as I continued, I realized this simple little task of tidying up could make the sleep even sweeter because I felt more at peace.

At night, tidying up my room was therapeutic. Even if the process was not always fun and I dreaded it at times, ultimately, it felt great.

Cleaning my room almost became a metaphor for cleaning my mind. It became a practice of self-care where I was purging the messiness from both my mind and my room.

I love for things to be clean and organized. For some reason being in a messy room gets me nervous and anxious because I feel my life isn't in my control. So, the challenge helped me feel better.

At night it was a signal for me to end my day and get ready to go to sleep. I would clean up the notebooks from my table, get my things ready for school, lay the blankets on my bed, and sleep peacefully.

As I often struggle to organize, this gave me a sense of clarity and order among the many things that I have. Also, since the bedroom is where I stay most of the time, this definitely helped make a more orderly environment.

I didn't think making my bed would honestly make that much of a difference but coming home to a made bed actually felt really good. Being tired, opening my door to a nicely made bed that was ready for me to jump into made it easy to wind down and fall asleep. It was surprising that just simply cleaning up my surroundings could have such a big difference in my emotions. Now, I really love making my bed.

Air Boxing

If I was stressed out or really mad at something and I just needed to take my mind off things, I'd do this challenge without a doubt. I listen to my favorite power songs and just punch to get my anger out of my system.

Before, I would hold these grudges; now I would get rid of the feelings by air boxing. Even though it was just an imaginary opponent, it helped me feel a lot better.

I would use this when I want to take revenge or imagine that I am punching a person that I want to punch (of course I never would in real life!).

When I have a lot of homework, this strategy helps me get through it and relieve my stress. Also, it would help motivate me because it reminds me that I can get through and beat out even the toughest challenges.

Conversation Starters

When I asked open-ended questions, I was able to have deeper conversations with people around me. For example, after I asked my dad an open-ended question, we talked for thirty minutes.

Getting out of my comfort zone to talk with other people was difficult but worth it.

The challenge made me feel significantly better after completing it because I had achieved something I hadn't done before, and I was able to talk to a wider variety of people than my usual friend group, which boosted my confidence a lot.

I had asked my dad to tell me about his first job, and he shared his memories of that job then memories from all his other jobs after that one. It was cool.

I believe that this challenge allowed me to improve my confidence and step out of my comfort zone as I tried to ask people that I usually don't talk to. With one simple question I get to know so much about a person.

5 Second Rule

The 5 second countdown was very effective because when I counted to five, it gave me a sense of urgency as if I had to get it done right away. I would use this strategy when I am feeling very lazy so that I can motivate myself to get things done.

Counting down was like a psychological device that helped me boost my concentration as well as starting tasks I didn't want to do. I wasn't stuck in a loop of procrastination when I used this technique.

Something about counting down, especially during moments when you just have to snap to focus, is incredibly helpful.

At first, I thought the challenge could be annoying since I had to act right away. However, I was able to finish everything a lot faster which meant I had more time to rest or do what I wanted to do. With this extra free time, I could relax, so the challenge proved to be very helpful.

It helped me wake up in the mornings instead of lagging and lingering which I usually do. Just counting down in my head to wake up was actually pretty helpful.

Guided Meditation

I would use this strategy in my everyday life especially if I had a stressful day or night and I just needed to wind down, relax, and sleep more comfortably and wake up feeling refreshed.

I loved the guided meditation before sleeping. It gave me a chance to gather myself and live in the moment. With guided meditation, I was able to be present at the moment and be aware of myself.

Although meditating for 30 minutes is not my thing, one minute each night before I sleep was a great way for me to start. Some nights I have so many stressful things on my mind that I cannot sleep for almost two hours. Doing guided meditation during those nights will definitely help me fall asleep faster.

The guided meditation was especially helpful the night before a big exam because it helped me relax and relieve the worries I usually have before a test. I'm always stressing and doubting myself, but the meditation helped put a lot of those thoughts away.

Act of Kindness

At first, I thought it would be annoying to help others. I thought to myself, it's hard enough trying to do everything I have to do, why do I need to help someone else as well? However, as I did the challenge over the week, my opinion changed. As other people appreciated my help, I saw why we were doing this. Spreading joy around me really helped me find the meaning behind this week's task and changed my perspective about the importance of being kind and helping others.

If you can do something that will help someone or create a smile on someone's face, then by all means do it. If there's a chance to do an act of kindness, seize it because you'll never regret it.

It always feels good to be of service because something small can go a long way for certain people, more than we might expect. I always try to keep that in mind.

I like this challenge because I felt good after seeing others feel good. Doing nice things also gave me a confidence boost because I stepped out of my comfort zone and did things that I usually don't do.

Aerobic Exercise

The aerobic exercise week made me feel energetic and happy, and dancing made me feel free and exhilarated because it's fun to dance, especially by yourself.

The obvious benefit is to my physical health because exercise is good for my heart and body. But it's also great for mental health because exercise lets me focus on being present in the moment, and I'm not anxious or worried about other things.

I would use this strategy if I were feeling a little drowsy that day. For example, if I got a lack of sleep the night before and was having a hard time staying up doing homework, I could run in place for a set amount of time to get my blood pumping and my mind awake.

I like sweating from doing the exercise, so this week's challenge was the perfect fit for me! Running releases endorphins to make me feel optimistic.

How Others See Me

It helped me gain more confidence and feel better about the way I see myself. I also now know some qualities that people admire about me I didn't know before.

Some words that I heard were surprising because I didn't think that was something they admired about me. My friend told me I was reliable, which was surprising because I didn't know they felt that way, and that made me really happy.

I was able to know how people see me and this made me understand what I mean to them.

Some of their words surprised me. For example, when someone pointed out that they admire my humor, I was surprised because I thought I was not a funny person and that was not one of my strengths, but I realized that I may be funny to other people even though I did not believe it for myself.

This challenge boosted my self-esteem as I felt more valued and honored when others complimented me. Also, it helped me strengthen my relationship with others, as I also shared what I admired about them when they told me what they admired about me.

After all of the words that I received about myself from other people, it changed the way I see myself. At first, I thought badly of myself in one area. However, after hearing good things about it from others, I thought that maybe I just thought worse of myself than what I actually am. This made me feel more confident in myself and realized that I am actually good at it.

Be in Nature

Early on, it was making me think about what I was doing with my time. After all, I could have been spending all that time doing homework or something "productive." But I took this time for self-care. It was a little slice of recharge and peace for the day.

I forgot how nice it is just to sit outside and look at all the green around me. I'm really thankful for this challenge because at some point through it I felt myself smiling unconsciously.

I felt the effects of this challenge immediately with my mental health and my overall well-being improving so much that it would be silly of me not to do it again.

It was hard at first to be away from my phone, and all the texts I couldn't respond to, but as time passed and I started focusing on nature, I thought about my phone less and less.

Being surrounded by the trees, wind, and all the natural sounds of the outside was a nice change from constantly being in front of a screen and hearing all the artificial buzz on my phone. I didn't hear the bustle of traffic or people, and taking time to disconnect was a refreshing and peaceful experience.

I just enjoyed the nice breeze and feeling of sunshine. I ended up just getting lost in thought and having an inner discussion with myself, which was nice.

Before, I felt overwhelmed and burdened by all the stresses I had from school and other responsibilities.

However, after being in nature, I felt a sense of relaxation, then noticed these problems were not as big as I thought they were.

I went hiking. I tried to notice every unique thing in nature such as the color of the wildflowers, the different types of trees and plants, and the cool and unique formation of rocks. Then, I laid down on the grass and looked up at the tall trees swaying and heard the leaves rustling as the slight breeze passed through them, and I felt at peace.

Hold a Plank

I wanted to try and take it upon as a true "challenge" in itself and try to improve my time. I used this challenge to start working out a little more, and I want to continue it so I can become more active in the summer. Mentally I felt accomplished and proud. It's a little thing, but I felt my own acknowledgment in the effort I put in.

Normally I only do planks for thirty seconds, but with this challenge, I was able to hold it for much longer and it shocked me. This challenge made me feel more physically fit and more mentally disciplined because I was pushing myself to hold a plank a little longer each day.

Every day I felt more and more accomplished with myself in holding a plank. Physically because I was getting myself to work out my abs and upper body strength, but it also helped me mentally because I had to keep an encouraging mindset to try to beat my last time.

This might sound weird, but I actually enjoy the pain I get from the exercise endurance. No pain, no gain! Therefore, this week was very fun and interesting to me.

Unplug Before Sleeping

Even though this was one of the hardest challenges I've done so far, I felt that this was the most effective on my mental and physical health because I was able to go to sleep without looking on social media and I ended up sleeping better.

I would do it when I'm tired, when I really need some self-control, or just want to have an electronic cleanse (like blocking myself out from the rest of the world).

Before, I noticed it took me a while to fall asleep so I was interested to see how this week's challenge would affect my sleeping routine. By unplugging, I got more sleep, and woke up more energized and well rested which means I wasn't waking up grumpy and taking it out on my family. And without my phone beside me when I woke up, I found myself making my bed, doing my skincare, and sometimes even making breakfast before checking it for updates. It made a big difference in my whole day.

Unplugging was so helpful. Just taking the time to focus on winding down at night and not having the light from my phone burn into my retinas felt good. I was able to fall asleep faster and get a better night of sleep. I usually go on my phone and then go to sleep, but this challenge showed me I felt better without it.

Decluttering

As I was decluttering my room, I was also decluttering my life in a way. For example, because my closet was so messy, I felt very unorganized and messy as well, but after I cleaned it out, I just felt more organized as a whole.

It was a real challenge having to get rid of something every day of the week because I LOVE collecting items for their sentimental value. Decluttering was almost like going through the stages of grief: sadness, stress, reflection, and then acceptance. I saw that the item didn't mean much in the end, it was the memory.

Any item that was old or had significant memories attached to it was hard to get rid of. I finally decided to let go of some of my stuffed animals and it was a real heartbreaker. But after a few days, I didn't even remember what I had discarded but I will always cherish the memories.

This is something that I've been putting off for a while since I had always been too lazy to throw things away or donate them, however, this challenge pushed me to start. It was hard for me to get rid of specific things, but, I thought, *'If I don't see myself with this in 5 years, then it's time to get rid of it.'*

I would do this again because it gives me the feeling of comfort and organization, which I love. It also calms my mind so I can focus on my work better.

Gratitude

I tend to complain a lot and criticize everything about myself and things around me. When this happens now, I will sit down and do this gratitude activity to remind myself of everything I am grateful for.

This challenge woke me up and reminded me that even though I might not be good at certain things, there are many things that I am capable of doing and I should be very grateful for that.

Gratitude is a way of encouraging positivity in life. I think practicing gratitude is something I can do more often in my life, like moments of reflection in these hectic moments.

Before my gratitude list, I would focus on the negative things. However, I read over my list and realized the number of things that I'm blessed to have.

Each day, I had so many things I was grateful for because I would think of one thing, which led me to remember another, and that would lead me to another.

I usually did this when I wasn't feeling very happy, and since I was thinking about what I am grateful for, it made me appreciate what I have and calmed me down. I thought about all the people that don't have what I think is "normal," which helped me appreciate life a lot more, and made me feel a lot better. It acts as a good reminder of how good we have it in life, and some people aren't lucky enough to have what we have, so purposefully writing things down and recognizing what you are grateful for is something that everyone should practice.

It was pretty easy for me to come up with many kinds of gratitude because I had a pretty clear vision of who I am thankful for, why I am thankful, and what I am thankful for. It was very entertaining to create this because I had so many smiles.

Choose Your Own Challenge

For our final week, the students designed their own challenge to complete, and their reflections were just as insightful as the previous weeks in the program.

Challenge: Reading and Interpreting Music Lyrics:
This challenge made me feel emotional at times. I was listening to a song and reading the lyrics, and I ended up relating to it so closely, it made me cry. I didn't realize that sometimes the songs that we listen to can hit so close to home and we can feel them on a deeper level when we slow down and read the lyrics.

Challenge: Running a Mile:
Before I started this challenge, I was scared because it was a MILE run. I was thinking this was something impossible to do. When I ran on the first day, I was struggling, but after I finished the whole week, I was able to see that everything is possible.

Challenge: Photographing Interesting Things:
The challenge made me feel better, as it made me feel happy and joyful when I looked at the photos that I took. Some of the photos were funny, while others were beautiful, as they were photos of nature, which is something I am fascinated and joyful about.

CHAPTER 19

Deeper Insights into the Findings

1. **Participants who were open and had a growth mindset saw better results.**

   Some were doubtful and resistant to participating in some of the challenges if they didn't think they would like them, or they didn't think they would be beneficial. However, the students who jumped in and did their best to complete the challenges and find their unique payoffs found many expected benefits, but also many unexpected ones. For example, those students who were open to charging their phones in another room instead of by their bed during the Unplug Before Sleeping challenge found their sleep improved, but also they remembered more of their dreams and had less daytime agitation and impatience. If students didn't want to unplug for the evenings, they did not see significant changes to the length of their sleep, quality of their sleep, or the brain activity during their sleep.

2. **Resilience and perseverance were up.**

   We measured their resilience and ability to overcome hard things, and everyone recorded improvement in thirty-three categories, with 80 percent of the girls measuring over 50 percent increases. In the post-assessment, the question with the biggest drop was *I feel stressed, anxious, nervous, or worried at some point every day*. The question with the highest increase was *I wake up feeling excited about my day most days of the week*. The third top answer which demonstrates resilience is: *I tend to bounce back quickly after hard times*. What these answers show us is after going through the IMPACT Project, the students have fewer negative emotions and thoughts, higher levels of joy and hopefulness, and a clear improvement in their resilience to recover from hard times in their lives.

3. Mindfulness Matters.

The top strategies selected by the students were in the Mindfulness category, followed by Connection to Others, Joyful Positivity, and Physical Activity. Their data, reflections, and discussions all showed that they feel life is demanding too much, moving too fast, and pushing them too hard. They crave simpler times, like being in nature, unplugging, and spending time in gratitude. When they had a moment to slow their thoughts and emotions down through challenges like Deep Breathing and Guided Meditation, they felt more grounded and recentered, giving them the energy to keep going. The responses to Deep Breathing and Guided Meditation illustrate how few times they experience peace and calm. After the IMPACT challenges, their answers to dealing with pressure and stress changed from ignoring their needs to scheduling activities to support their needs with quality self-care activities like hiking in the forest, spending time with books or listening to music, or spending quality time with their family and friends. If their lives were stormy and tumultuous, they were especially drawn to creating a gratitude list or being quiet in nature.

4. Moving From Motionless to Motion.

Teens are emotionally, mentally, and intellectually exhausted and it often takes a big push to move their bodies if they are not in organized sports at school or in after school programs. Sir Isaac Newton's First Law of Motion stated that, 'A body in motion stays in motion, and a body at rest, stays at rest.' For those not in sports, they resisted exercise until we introduced challenges that required movement. Once they overcame their mental resistance, they enjoyed moving their bodies in both easy ways, like stretching, and in challenging ways, like holding a plank longer each day. One of the best ways we found to spark their movement was to make the physical activity challenge short and purposeful so they could get the quick rush of 'happy' neurotransmitters and feel better without too much sweat. The highest ranked physical activity challenge was completing an aerobic exercise, and the second was holding a plank for as long as possible. Both of these challenges were favorites because of the opportunity to compete against themselves and outperform their previous record each day. That slight gamification increased their competitiveness and joy inspired them to engage fully.

5. **Students craved connection with like-minded people sharing similar interests.**

Most of the students in the study didn't know each other at all, yet everyone showed up every Sunday night for five months, even though our project ran during the school year, through several blocks of exams, college placement exams, sports tournaments, and family celebrations. In our post-assessment, we learned that 100 percent of our students ranked our Sunday night meetings as the best part of the program, with 90 percent of the students ranking the actual 'doing of the challenges' as second best. We wondered why, and through our analysis, we saw that students craved connection with others. They had found a safe space to have open, honest discussions about stress and overwhelm, and felt empowered to continue to break the stigma and shame around mental health. In our post-Covid world, they craved more meaningful conversations, more trust and openness, and deeper relationships with their family and friends - new and old. However, most of the students in this study had underdeveloped social skills or deep introversion tendencies, and only one of the students considered themselves an extrovert. Completing challenges like Act of Kindness, Compliment Others or Conversation Starters were quite uncomfortable and unnerving for most students because these activities required them to move outside of their comfort zone. However, we found something interesting. Even though they felt awkward, they did it anyway because they wanted to complete the challenges. When we asked them to share about their experiences, many students reported that when they made the effort to connect on a deeper level with their friends or family, two things happened. First, all the students found so much personal value in the deeper conversations with their friends or family, and the conversations lasted longer. Second, they learned more about the other person in one conversation with open-ended questions or by starting with a compliment than in all their previous conversations. Relationships are really important, especially deep, connected ones, and learning tools and techniques to deepen those connections made a big difference for the students.

6. **When given the choice, students chose activities that they had a desire to try.**

Students found Choose Your Own Challenge to be very beneficial and enjoyable. Having gone through seventeen previous challenges, they were able to assess what other mindful or self-awareness practice they wanted to test in the parameters of the program, and then commit to completing their choice in the same fashion as all the previous challenges. This increase in self-awareness helped with their decision-making abilities. We believe that the Choose Your Own Challenge was also highly ranked because they had more clarity around what kind of activities supported their mental health and wellness better than others. In fact, many of the students chose an activity that was similar to their favorite challenge overall. For example, one participant found the planking challenge really inspiring and empowering, and the Choose Your Own Challenge was completing more and more push-ups every day. This student knew what motivated him and wanted to test this new activity in the same physical exercise category. That is quality self-awareness!

7. Family placement influenced student outcomes.

There is a lot of research about the validity of family placement as a variable in studies. We looked at family placement data each week to evaluate for statistical significance, and almost always, we found relevance. In our study, we had students who were the oldest child in their family, the middle child, the youngest child, and an only child. Of the eighteen challenges, there was one challenge that scored the highest for every student, and that was Be in Nature. For the other seventeen challenges, we found some interesting trends. The oldest children in our study found mindfulness challenges, such as Guided Meditation and Gratitude, most helpful. We believe this may be due to these students carrying the heaviest load among the children in their family to help their parents, care for or manage younger siblings, and complete extra household chores. For the students who are middle and youngest children, they ranked the How Others See Me Challenge highest (after Be in Nature), signifying that they are more insecure or uncertain about their value compared to the oldest and need confirmation or validation. The only children ranked the Choose Your Own Challenge in their top three because it's likely that they are used to making decisions for themselves and feel comfortable taking ownership of their experience.

8. Grade trends showed significant growth in self-awareness and self-care.

At the beginning of the project, we saw the students had significant stress around grades daily; we learned how their focus on perfect grades led to their persistent fear of failure, test anxiety, performance anxiety, procrastination followed by panic, and dread around high stakes tests and exams.

We had two objectives with grades. First, we acknowledged their state of stress-overload and we wanted to find the mindfulness strategies that helped reduce the most stress in the least amount of time. Second, we wanted to teach tools that would directly impact how they could manage ongoing stress better.

In an answer to the first objective, we found that collectively, the students ranked Be in Nature, Choose Your Own, Gratitude, and Unplug Before Sleeping as their top four most effective strategies. However, upon deeper reflection, we realized that the distribution of students in each grade level impacted the results. When we broke the numbers down by grade, freshmen students (9th grade) ranked Conversation Starters highest, likely because transitioning from middle school to high school is a difficult period which can cause heightened social anxiety, especially in a post-COVID world. As they are new to social networking and building new friendships, challenges that encouraged them to connect with others on a deeper level benefitted them significantly.

As for the upper grade students, they ranked Mindfulness challenges such as Be in Nature and Guided Meditation the highest. This is likely because of their higher reported scores on stress. As the academic pressures weigh more heavily on their shoulders in the later years of high school, the expectations on them become bigger and heavier. Therefore, taking time to slow things down, recenter themselves, and regain their focus by having a clearer mind helped them the most and gave them the strength to push through. They also reported a higher positive shift in stress management, better sleep, and reduced anxiety with these strategies.

In an answer to the second objective, we found that it was a combination between mindfulness techniques and leadership training that led to the biggest difference. Not only did students learn how to decompress from stress once they were feeling it, but they also learned how to spot the signs early, and notice patterns of behavior which often led to increased stress, like procrastination or time mismanagement.

Since the students were laser-focused on grades and performance, we tracked their grades and recorded them before and after the study. We saw that the number of students whose grades stayed the same did not change from before the study to the end of the study. Interestingly, the number of grades that increased and the number of grades that decreased were equal.

What was one unexpected result? We expected the students with decreased grades to experience a negative mental health impact based on the prolific reporting of students' stress and panic around grades in the pre-assessment. However, that wasn't the case at all. Every student, including those whose grades went down, reported that they were less stressed, overwhelmed, anxious or worried on a daily basis. They also ranked other things higher than grades, like nurturing friendships, taking care of their needs, finding balance, prioritizing sleep, and being happy. One conclusion we could make is that students felt less stress around grades because they had shifted their mindset to acknowledge that their worth and value did not come from achieving a specific *grade*. As well, through our discussions and trainings, we were able to demonstrate that their 'mistakes' were not failures at all, but opportunities to learn more about what worked, what didn't work, and what new ideas they could test. In this study, they put their perfectionism tendencies and self-criticism under the microscope and saw it wasn't healthy mentally, emotionally, or physically, and made life-changing shifts in search of better balance.

9. Did gender play a role?

The gender breakdown of our participants was five girls, six boys, and everyone identified with the gender of their birth. From the first week, we noticed patterns that were emerging between the two genders in some of the challenges, but not others. For example, both boys and girls overall ranked Be in Nature as their highest-scored, most impactful challenge. Then the data diverges. Here is one example.

Everyone acknowledges feeling insecure is universal; they wonder whether they are liked by others, whether they are being judged, whether others notice their imperfections. This becomes a constant guessing game because they are left to guess how others view them. We tested their self-perception in the "How Others See Me" challenge, where they had the opportunity to ask directly how others thought of them.

The girls shared how much pressure society places on girls to look a certain way to fit into an unrealistic standard of beauty. They shared that asking others to answer this week's challenge question was extremely uncomfortable and nerve-wracking. The girls admitted they typically attribute their own level of self-worth from the feedback they receive from others, and since they didn't know how others perceived them, opening up to possible judgment or criticism was scary. This challenge was transformative because it elicited a burst of emotions when they heard the positive, generous, uplifting words from family and friends; they were truly surprised when no one pointed out their self-identified 'shortcomings, flaws, or imperfections.' The girls also reported a greater increase in confidence and happiness knowing that they are not negatively judged by their friends. For all our students, learning that they are valued and loved for who they are and not who they think they should be significantly attributed to their self-esteem and confidence.

Another example of how the data diverged between the boys and the girls is where the numbers showed that the boys ranked physical activities in their top three, and the girls ranked physical activities in their lowest three. Also, many of the boys chose a physical activity for their Choose Your Own Challenge in Week 18, whereas for the same challenge, the girls chose activities like taking pictures of things that make them happy, and listening to songs while reading the lyrics so they could understand the songs in a deeper way.

While this data does not represent the preferences of *all girls* or *all boys*, it does shed light on the need for self-determination in mental health and wellness practices. It was very clear that the boys found great stress relief in big muscle movements like hiking, running, planking, and weightlifting, and the girls chose quiet mindfulness and deepening relationships to others as being their best strategies for managing stress.

10. Teens and technology

Today's teens cannot imagine a world without their laptops and smartphones. There are too many buzzes, bings, and notifications from all directions to even know what peace and quiet feels like. Even if they turn off their device, their habits are so deeply established that they always want to be checking what their friends are posting or their favorite celebrities are doing, often without thinking.

Our findings showed us that even if they never thought about the power of their phone and the relentless pull of their online world before, doing some of the technology-distancing challenges opened their eyes to their technology habits pretty quickly. And, once the shock of being phone-free for a short period of time lessened, all of the students really appreciated the peace and freedom they felt without having it with them or on all the time.

Overall, the challenge that was ranked the highest was the Be in Nature Challenge. This didn't just require them to be in nature, they needed to be friend-free and phone-free too. We emphasized how wild and wondrous the world could be if they experienced it through their five senses: we asked them to look all around them, listen for the sounds, touch the textures, and smell the scents (please note, we didn't encourage any wild tastings!) Another requirement of this challenge was that it lasted at least thirty minutes, which was much longer than any other challenge. For many, the first five minutes were the hardest because they love their phones, and heavily rely on them like lifelines to their friends and the world around them. But once the five minute mark passed, they started to settle into their environment and found how grand and amazing it was, like one student said, 'it was like a slice of heaven.' They reported peace and calm feelings, as well as having the mental space to think about their life, their friendships or relationships, or other big questions.

A second challenge that ranked high on the overall list was Unplug Before Sleeping. This challenge required them to power down thirty minutes before bed and charge their devices somewhere else instead of in their room, or beside their bed. We found that the students who kept their phone near them had a much harder time resisting the pull of checking the latest updates or posts, and those who charged their device in another part of their home had an easier time finding other things to do, like reading, tidying up, and spending more time and intention on their self-care or nighttime routines.

Another outcome the students experienced was around their sleep - quality and quantity. During the week they unplugged and powered down, they reported an increase in the amount of sleep they got each night, as well as a better quality sleep. They were more rested and had better attitudes, patience, focus, and energy during the days. Even though they reported such positive outcomes, they weren't sure if they would power down and unplug from their devices every night because they didn't like being disconnected from their friends and family, but they all said they would try to find a solution that fit their needs best.

We all have devices and can recognize the power they hold over us: endless entertainment options, updates from friends, sales from our favorite stores, and the latest news about things we care about. However, in our discussions, our group talked about the 'cost of connecting online' in our friendships and relationships. This topic was even more relevant because these students had recently experienced online or remote learning for months, or even a year, because of the global pandemic, and they knew it didn't feel the same as being in a classroom with their peers and teacher. As we proceeded through the program, we introduced various challenges that helped the students increase their interactions with their friends and family in person, and they saw yet another example of how much more authentic and engaged they felt in person, versus online. This generation, or any generation for that matter, is not suddenly going to drop technology altogether, but perhaps they will think twice before texting the person right beside them, instead of asking the question out loud.

Overall, teens and technology are forever intertwined. However, they all report now that they have seen how automatic and prevalent their phones are in their lives, they will be more mindful to unplug and be phone-free during some activities. They will hopefully remember that when they were away from their devices, they felt better, more relaxed, less insecure, more rested, and less anxious, and they can embrace tech-free times as part of their day.

11. Transformation Before Our Eyes

When we talk with parents, they often share how hard it is to motivate one teen to do extra work, especially if it *feels* like work. They often remarked that they have no idea how we motivated eleven teens to test, track, document, and reflect deeply in written form every week for five months, answering hundreds of questions about their thoughts, feelings, and fears, on top of everything else they manage in their lives.

The answer isn't as hard as one might think. We asked our students to look at what their life could look like if they weren't so stressed, overwhelmed, exhausted, angry, or fearful. Then we asked them to step into becoming leaders in their lives, assessing where they are, envisioning where they want to be, and creating a plan that honors their mental, emotional, and physical needs to get there.

To their surprise, being a leader has nothing to do with the title you hold and has everything to do with the impact you want to make with your skills, abilities, passions, and vision. One of our key findings was that the IMPACT Project helped them identify their skills, abilities, and passions, and encouraged them to set a vision for their future that they could work towards.

As well, every week we reinforced how many ways they could step into leadership as there wasn't one way for everyone. This seemed to open the creative floodgates for our students.

From Quiet to Confident: How the IMPACT Project launched a legacy of leadership.

Two IMPACT students met for the first time in our program but quickly discovered they both wanted to keep the conversation around mental health going. They decided to launch a new podcast called *"Many Ways to Be Okay,"* based on their experiences in the program, and their desire to continue to break the stigma around mental health for teens. They are currently building their own website to support the podcast and their upcoming blog.

Several students attended intensive summer camps or mission trips in different cities or states to further develop ways they can positively impact others.

One student took the initiative to create a website to create a community of like-minded musicians to have discussions about music and share musical inspiration.

Several students started working in sports coaching and health care where they could continue being of service to others and make a positive impact.

One student coached girls in a digital coding camp and is designing and launching two digital courses on how to make a podcast and build a website.

The students had the opportunity to end their participation in the program after the challenge section, but every single one of them wanted to stay and work for another two months on brainstorming, drafting, editing, and finalizing a chapter for this book. In our pre-assessment, many students mentioned they wanted to write a book someday but didn't believe they could, and through this experience, they have met this incredible life goal. True leaders!

CHAPTER 20

What's Next

We have given you a sampling of eighteen of the best self-care, stress-management, and mental health support strategies out there. Take what works, test it with your teen, and help them discover what works for them, and when it works best. Remember, not every strategy will work every time the same way. You need many different tools at your disposal. We offered four categories to our students: mindfulness, joyful positivity, connection to others, and physical activity. We did this because we need choices, we need options. You won't use the same technique to manage your job loss as you do your car being totaled by a meteor. Having many tools available means you are ready, regardless of the storm that comes your way.

Preparing your teen with a wide variety of tools sets them up for success in their academics, relationships, sports or club competitions, and interactions in their community. Even after finding a good number of effective strategies to support your teen in many different ways, it's important to encourage them to stay open to new ideas. As they mature, they may find some of the tools less effective, so being in a growth- mindset around mental health will ensure they always know to look for options to support them in their times of need.

Also, refer back to our list every so often and see if something that might not have worked before could work now. Our students thought some of the challenges wouldn't be effective at all, yet found deep transformation in making their bed, or air boxing, or putting their phone in another room during the night.

Mental health is a complex web that runs through all parts of our lives, touching on who we are, how we feel about ourselves, how we feel about others, and what we think we can achieve in our lives. Nurture your mental health and model good self-care so your teens, and everyone else around you, can see how healthy mind, body, and soul come to be.

CHAPTER 21

Our Final Thoughts

For all of us, when we face trials and tribulations, stresses and struggles, or challenges and conflicts, one question is fundamental to every stressful, difficult or uncomfortable experience: what will help me through it?

When we embarked on this research project, we wanted to empower students to talk about their experiences, share their journey, and help us break the stigma around mental health.

Every culture and every region has their own understanding of mental health, but so does every stage in life. Many teens don't talk about feelings because it makes them feel awkward or inadequate. So, we asked, why? Why was it so hard for teens to talk about feelings or emotions?

Some teens said they thought mental health was reserved for people with mental illnesses, some thought there was no point since no one really cared, some thought talking about their stress or struggle showed they were ungrateful for all they had, and some others thought talking about it revealed a person's weakness and was something that brought shame.

We know these are some of the reasons there is a stigma around mental health, and this is also why we were so passionate to bring the topic of mental health and wellness out into the open.

We wanted to change the way people think and feel about mental health, and we wanted to impact the next generation of leaders and influencers. We wanted it to be more than just an education in mental health; we wanted to change their lives and empower them to change other people's lives and be part of a movement to normalize mental health and wellness across cultures, generations, and locations.

As we talked about mental health in our weekly discussions, we normalized both struggles and solutions to show the students that *no one is the only one* experiencing stresses, strains, or struggles. Through our insightful conversations, as well as what we saw in various stories, videos, and articles in our program, we showed that everyone faces mental health challenges in their lives, all throughout their lives. Because stress, overwhelm, and pressure touches everyone, it's on each of us to break the stigma and start the shift.

Teens talk about many things, but the inner workings of their human experience tends not to be top of their list. We worked to change this. We often spoke about how it was okay to not be okay, and our students heard us loud and clear as demonstrated by two participants in the IMPACT Project who are launching a podcast called, "Many Ways to be Okay."

In 2022, we are starting to see the shifts in the greater society as well. More teens are driving the movement to reduce the stigma around mental health. The vast majority of teens surveyed by the National 4-H Council agreed that "as a culture, we should embrace both the ups and downs of mental health; it's okay to feel bad sometimes."

The idea that nine teens from the Korean culture, widely seen as a culture that struggles deeply with mental health suffering and stigma, can come together to even have the conversation, plus change the conversation, gives us great hope. With care, confidence, and commitment, mental health stigmas can be dismantled in every culture.

Tony Robbins said, "The quality of life is the quality of your emotions." By breaking the stigma, we can name our emotions, process them, and release the ones that don't serve our greater good. And, it all starts with talking, listening, and learning.

Our teens wouldn't have tried most of these challenges without having the guidance, encouragement, and support of a group of people wanting to know how to move from overwhelmed to overjoyed, or from a place of chaos to a place of calm. If your teen seeks support in their personal growth journey, seek out like-minded people and help them get plugged into the group. Except for four people, our students didn't know each other before the study, yet, through this experience, they made friends, they found answers, they realized they weren't alone, and they had people around who could listen to their experience and help them move through it to a place of understanding. We hope you have clubs, groups, or teams in your community where your teen can connect to others and step into their authentic brilliance. As always, they are welcome to join the next IMPACT Project and discover their own strategies for success and transformation.

We hope that our research project has sparked some ideas for you along the way, helping you build your awareness of your stresses and struggles, and testing new solutions to move through them when they storm into your life. Maybe there are some challenges our students tested that you want to test for yourself, or maybe you have some ideas that you always wanted to test but haven't done so yet. Our advice is to do it and pay attention to how you feel, not what you think. Our brains will resist most changes, even if they are good for us.

We saw incredible transformations for our students, and we wish the same for you. Please keep this list of challenges handy for a time when you are feeling overwhelmed, trapped, stressed out, or struggling, and you need to find a way to get through your storm before you get pushed to your own breaking point. Thirty years ago, I watched James's crash when he hit his breaking point. Sitting with him in the bathtub, trying to stop the bleeding shook me to my core, and changed me in deep and profound ways. Promise me, you will never let it get that far. Use our IMPACT Project as a framework to build your own selection of helpful, healthy strategies to help you know your strengths, know your boundaries, and invest every day in activities and practices that recognize and honor your physical, emotional, and mental health. Every part of you deserves love and attention, and when you are committed to giving it to yourself, you won't let yourself down.

CHAPTER 22

Final Quotes from Our Teens

I've always heard of self-care days, but I never really understood the power of them because I didn't think it would be effective to add in these little routines to help myself. But now, I've learned that the first step to improving mental health doesn't have to come from outside first, but rather a change in my own mindset to take action to relieve myself of my own anxiety.

We broke down the stigma of mental health by talking about it and knowing we can get through our struggles by using the things that we learned. We now know many little things we can do to manage our stress and take care of ourselves. We validated the idea that it's okay to not be okay all the time, as long as we know what we can do about it, and how to use the resources available to us when we are stuck.

Mental health was always a very important topic for me. I was in therapy before because I wanted to better myself. The topic of mental health shouldn't be something to be embarrassed about because we all go through things, and going through things is normal. After taking a part in this project, my view and knowledge towards mental health has expanded. I now know more about myself, and I hope our book gives that opportunity to everybody else as well.

Before the project I defined mental health, like always feeling stressed and unhappy, as an issue with the brain. Going through the challenges and the entire project, I view it as something that can be changed and improved with simple changes to my lifestyle. One thing that hasn't changed is how important mental health is, and that's why I'm trying to break the stigma around it.

My understanding and knowledge of mental health were very little before the project. After experiencing the IMPACT Project, learning more about mental health, and doing the challenges, I now know that there is so much more to mental health. It's not only feelings and emotions, but mental health can affect things like confidence, concentration, motivation, friendships and social life, and many more. I also learned that mental health can be changed by many things as well, and having mindfulness, connection, and physical activity challenges showed me that as well. Mental health is different for every person, and it's up to us to find the helpful things to support our wellness. And, even though it's up to us, we don't have to do it all alone. Find like-minded people and support each other, it makes the journey even better.

CHAPTER 23
Mental Health Resources

National Alliance on Mental Health (NAMI) nami.org

The Hope Line www.thehopeline.com

Mental Health America www.mhanational.org

Active Minds www.activeminds.org

Bring Change to Mind www.bringchange2mind.org

BeWellLine www.bewellline.com

For more information about the IMPACT Project, or to join us in the next program, please contact us through our website at www.startyourimpact.com.

Made in the USA
Las Vegas, NV
11 June 2023

73291861R00118